STUFF THAT MAKES
A GAY HEART WEEP

A DEFINITIVE GUIDE TO THE

LOUD & PROUD

DISLIKES OF MILLIONS

freeman hall

Adamsmedia

AVON, MASSACHUSETTS

Published by
Adams Media, a division of F+W Media, Inc.
57 Littlefield Street, Avon, MA 02322. U.S.A.
www.adamsmedia.com

ISBN 10: 1-4405-0655-8
ISBN 13: 978-1-4405-0655-0
eISBN 10: 1-4405-1034-2
eISBN 13: 978-1-4405-1034-2

Printed in the United States of America.

10 9 8 7 6 5 4 3 2 1

Library of Congress Cataloging-in-Publication Data
is available from the publisher.

This publication is designed to provide accurate and authoritative information
with regard to the subject matter covered. It is sold with the understanding that the publisher is not engaged in rendering legal, accounting, or other
professional advice. If legal advice or other expert assistance is required, the
services of a competent professional person should be sought.
   —From a *Declaration of Principles* jointly adopted by a Committee of the
American Bar Association and a Committee of Publishers and Associations

Many of the designations used by manufacturers and sellers to distinguish
their product are claimed as trademarks. Where those designations appear
in this book and Adams Media was aware of a trademark claim, the designations have been printed with initial capital letters.

Uncredited photos copyright © Freeman Hall.

This book is available at quantity discounts for bulk purchases.
For information, please call 1-800-289-0963.

DEDICATION

To weeping gay hearts everywhere—you are not alone.

ACKNOWLEDGMENTS

No weeping here, only gratitude and thanks for all these people who helped show the world what gay hearts weep over: Wendy Simard and Holly Root. Gay heart photo models and helpers: Jeff Swan, Billee Burchett, Krystine Chaparro, Ossie Beck, Danusha Kibby, Vanessa Schafer, Christiana Glasner, Nancy Foster, Betty Gomez, Kari DelMastro, Theresa Bozek, Kylie Bozek, Sarah Melland, Mimi, Walt Kibby, Daiva Venckus, Peta Russell, Fred Chaparro, Bill Bozek, Cassie Bozek, Chelsea Bozek, Lee and Dave Marquardson, Shoushan. Gay heart inspiration from: Michelle Quevedo, Craig Questa, Andrew Zieser, Michael Jameson, Benjamin Kissell, Beach Weston, Sherina Florence, Julie Darling, Ken Arlitz, Jane Summer, Brandy Rivers, Calindy Mann, Gina Mae Temelcoff, AfterElton.com. And thank you to these cat and dog models: Arion the Bichon (Snuggie model), Simba (Wii Fit Model), Lanie (Bumble Bee Costume model), and Dede (*Jesus Camp* model).

CONTENTS

♡ ₁ BAD DRAG

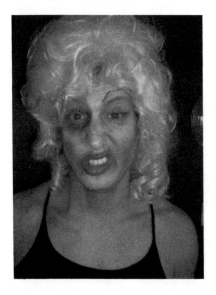

From RuPaul to Miss Coco Peru, gay hearts adore eye-popping, outrageous fashionista drag queens dripping with snarky fabulous attitude. What they weep over is suddenly finding themselves in a slasher film, cornered in a bar by a scary drunk in bad drag with sweaty cracked makeup, smeared lipstick, and ratty cigarette-smelling hair, wearing horrible thrift store clothes, ripped stockings, and cheap broken stilettos. Gay hearts weep in total horror at bad drag and run for the nearest exit, screaming like Jamie Lee Curtis in *Halloween*.

WEEPY DRAG QUEEN NAME GENERATOR

Maybe you can't be as dragalicious as RuPaul's drag queens, but you can have your own drag name that you can use in online chat rooms and to give to creeps at bars or aggressive telemarketers. To make your drag name, do the following steps.

1. TAKE YOUR FIRST NAME AND:

If you are a dude	Change it to a colorful chick's name: Andrew becomes Amber, Sam becomes Suzi, Chuck becomes Chi Chi, etc.
If you are a chick, you can either	Use your first name (make sure it's totally femmed, a little odd, and over the top: Susan becomes Sofonda, Patty becomes Peaches, etc.).
OR	Choose any of the following: Candy, Coco, Ursula, Shantay, Hedda, Alexis, Trixie, Porsche, Angel, Tammy, or Lady.

2. TAKE YOUR NEW FIRST NAME AND ADD IT TO ANY OF THESE NAMES:

Divine	Peru
Boom Boom	Cocks
Diamond	Sunbeam
Sextoy	LaRue
Fetish	Hedwig
Lypsinka	Uranus

And now you have your very own drag name. Just don't forget to add Miss in front of it!

FACEBOOK GIFTS

Like billions of other people, gay hearts cannot get enough of Facebook. They love posting photos of their lunch, finding old high school enemies, stalking former lovers, and collecting millions of friends. What they don't love, however, is Facebook gifts. Gay hearts liken a Facebook gift to that of a greeting card without any money or gift cards inside. It sucks, it's lame, and it makes a gay heart weep because what the hell are they going to do with the image of a dandelion, empty shot glass, lava lamp, roll of toilet paper, ham hock, half eaten corn dog, sock on a doorknob or a thong with a bow on the front? Delete it. That's what they're going to do. If you plan on sending a gay heart a Facebook gift of a virtual BMW 3 Series Coupe, you had better make for damn sure that the keys to a real one are right behind it.

⟨3⟩ ♡ CHEAP BOOZE

When gay hearts get trashed and have blackout sex, they want to do it with the finest liquors available. Not the $5.99 grocery store watered-down vodka that tastes like it was distilled in the sewers of Romania.

To keep gay hearts happy, always liquor them up with the finest: Grey Goose, Jack Daniels, Jäger-meister, Opus One, Cristal, or Sam Adams. This way they can achieve obnoxious drunken behavior with the kind of memorable glory that will have them saying things they would never say, dancing and singing in places they would never be caught dancing and singing, and eventually becoming lost on the streets, finally vomiting in a ficus tree planter in front of some random office building. Good gay times for all. Of course, then there are the delusional gay hearts who believe drinking only the best booze greatly reduces their odds of being tagged in embar-rassing photos on Facebook.

Gay hearts also weep every time they get a drink at a bar or event with a not-so-generous portion of their chosen spirit. Bartenders, listen up. You want a big tip? Make your gay-heart customer's eyes water. They will reward you.

And just to be clear, while gay hearts may weep over cheap booze, they will *never* turn it down.

4 ♥ A TOWN WITHOUT TARGET, TRADER JOE'S, OR WHOLE FOODS

. . . is a town no gay heart could ever call home. Or even visit, for that matter. For gay hearts, living in a town with no Target, Trader Joe's, or Whole Foods would be like an end-of-the-world science fiction movie right before everyone turns to cannibalism. They'd starve, have nothing to wear, and nothing cool in their homes. They wouldn't be able to text their lover and say, "Hey, I'm going to Targé, TJ's, and Whole. You need anything?" The naked, hungry gay heart would weep uncontrollably until it had to drive hundreds of miles away in search of the bull's-eye beacon and that undeniable Whole Foods smell.

♡5 SARAH PALIN

Sarah Palin doesn't just make gay hearts weep; she scares the shit out of them. They are afraid she will take over the planet and send all gay hearts to Alaska, force them to live in log cabins, wear ugly hunting clothes, remain single without benefits, and become slaves to building her bridge to Russia, which she will secretly use as a one-way gay super highway to deport gays out of America.

Although fearful of a Sarah Palin administration, on the other hand gay hearts can't get enough of lampooning her. Watching *SNL*'s Tina Fey impersonations, dressing up as her for Halloween, and going to a Sarah Palin stripper contest are all ways the gay heart can laugh away the weepiness she causes.

⟨6⟩ MANBOOBS

While trying not to vomit, a gay heart weeps for men with gelatinous, saggy breasticles. They pray Beverly Hills plastic surgeon Dr. Robert Rey (aka *Dr. 90210*) will answer the call to rid the world of this terrible affliction by offering free manboob reductions. Bitchtits and the men that show them off must be stopped.

ANYTHING HAVING TO DO WITH *TWILIGHT*

Vampire mania has thrown the planet off its bloodsucking axis and gay hearts everywhere are weeping bloody tears over the popularity of everything *Twilight*.

Stephenie Meyer's lobotomizing soapy books have spawned cheesy and terrible movies, actors and actresses who look and sound gay but supposedly aren't, ghastly hair styles, and so much appalling buzz, gay hearts are so over seeing Robert Pattinson's mug all over billboards, magazine covers, and ridiculous merch. Do people *really* need to wipe their butts with *Twilight*-themed toilet paper?

With the exception of HBO's *True Blood*, gay hearts stand united in saying that there is only one saga of vampires that rules the world and it was created by the Queen of Vampires, Anne Rice.

The immortal truth: Lestat could kick Edward's ass.

With his eyes closed.

8 ♡ CROCS

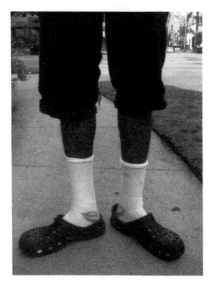

A gay heart weeps instantly at the sight of Crocs. It cannot understand why an atrociously ugly clog-shaped plastic shoe with holes in it could become so outrageously popular. And why on earth would anyone want to wear shoes that could kill them if they decide to take an escalator to the second floor of the mall?

Although the popularity of Crocs has waned in recent years, there are those who refuse to remove their feet from them and have taken to wearing socks with their crocs. This makes a gay heart weep even more and possibly gag a little.

Even though many gay hearts claim to be 100 percent on board to support the growing STOP WEARING CROCS movement and they will vocally shred their Croc-wearing friends to pieces, saying things like "Crocs are hideous, why in gay hell are you wearing them? Take them off!" there's a dark side to this anti-Croc support. Once these supposed Croc haters get home and lock their front door, they are secretly slipping on a pair of bright yellow Crocs themselves (with or without socks) and lounging all over the house in them, and doing everything from gardening to having sex in them. These Croc-wearing hypocrites will never admit they own Crocs in a million years and will never be seen wearing them in public.

But the gay-heart truth is this: Plastic shoes with holes in them were meant for Barbie dolls, *not* people.

NO VALET SERVICE

Nothing is more aggravating to a gay heart than having to spend precious time looking for a parking space. Because gay hearts are often late for concerts and dinner reservations, opting for valet service is a no-brainer, and they will think nothing of spending $20 just so they don't have to drive around in circles. If no valet service is found and the only parking seems miles away, a gay heart will weep like a baby and possibly just look for a new restaurant or park illegally for a concert (thus considering the ticket fee as the cost of parking). It's not that gay hearts don't like to walk—they love long hikes, traipsing all over an amusement park, or shopping all day at the mall. They just don't like walking to their cars.

♡ 10 SCARY SEX TOYS

Some gay boys and some gay girls love to spice up their sex lives with adult toys. A $75 Jeff Stryker latex dildo or a $90 Thrusting Jack Rabbit vibrator with an extra-strong piston can be good times in the bedroom with a partner or alone with the cats and dogs sitting nearby watching uninterested. However, when the sex toys start to look like freakish alien anal probes, the gay heart weeps like a scared little bitch, defiantly saying, you are not putting that thing anywhere near my bum or vajayjay.

11 PEOPLE WHO DON'T LIKE TO BE CALLED HON, SWEETIE, OR GIRL

Gay hearts weep with speechless frustration when they meet someone who corrects them after they've addressed her by saying "Hon," "Sweetie," or "Girl." Most of the people who don't like being called "hon," "sweetie," or "girl" are robotic straight women on power trips afraid of showing any kind of feminine emotion. Gay hearts weep for these people because even though they will try their hardest to oblige the formal request in an accommodating way, using "hon," "sweetie," or "girl" comes naturally for gay hearts and is part of their genetic makeup. Attempting to edit "hon" or "sweetie" usage for any prolonged time could cause a gay heart to snap like *Glee's* cranky head coach Sue Sylvester. The second they approach with a "Hey girl," and their new acquaintance corrects them with a condescending, "My name is not 'girl,'" the gay hearts won't be able to hold back from answering, "How about if I call you bitch instead?"

TERMS TO USE INSTEAD OF HON, SWEETIE, OR GIRL

Hey You!

Man

Dude

Bitch or Douche

Lover

Sir or Ma'am

Pumpkin

Governor

Babe

Darling

Gorgeous

Cupcake

Sweet Cheeks

OVERPRICED CUPCAKES

Cupcakes have taken the world by scrumptious storm! And gay hearts have gone cupcake crazy eating them for breakfast, lunch, dinner, and any time in between. They love cupcake towers at a birthday party loaded with red velvet covered in luscious cream cheese frosting and fondant hearts or devouring a batch of chocolate fudge whipped up at home after an ugly break up. Yes, for a gay heart, a cupcake brightens their day and puts a smile on their face. However when the cupcake craving hits and a gay heart encounters an overpriced boutique called Mrs. Prissy's Cupcakes selling $5 cupcakes looking like mini-muffins with a dollop-sized squirt of icing on top, the weeping begins, because they know, in their gayest of gay hearts, that they will probably have to buy two, if not three, of the designer cupcakes to satisfy their sweet tooth's desire.

SCARY PACKAGES

Gay male hearts are avid crotch watchers. Underwear or commando, a nice fist-sized lump or a banana-shaped silhouette will leave them delirious with wanting to know what's behind the enticing bulge. But when they see a dude out in public freeballin' and their junk looks all ballooned-out and infected in the shape of a warped football, there is nothing to do but weep in gay horror. And run away from the dick tumor very very fast.

14 ♡ TAP WATER

It's no secret that gay hearts will do anything to avoid drinking tap water. They would rather guzzle warm goat milk, or simply pass out from dehydration, than have to swig water directly from a kitchen or bathroom sink. You will also never spot a gay heart sipping from a public water fountain or garden hose. Many will not even drink from glasses served at restaurants because they are not sure where the water came from. For some gay hearts, water filters are acceptable; however, most prefer their water directly out of a labeled, beautifully crafted plastic bottle. Water they can trust.

NOUVELLE CUISINE

Make no mistake about it—gay hearts LOVE to eat amazing food! And many of them are just as passionate about cooking. They love fine dining, hole-in-the-wall diners, trendy hot spots, and fun sushi places. They love making late-night after-clubbing fast-food runs, meeting up for brunch the next afternoon, discovering the world's best pizza or hot dog, and trying a new Asian/Italian fusion place that just opened. (Gay hearts will try any new food concept at least once! Even if it makes no sense.)

But what makes the gay heart weep in the food world is nouvelle cuisine. While many gay hearts enjoy watching *Top Chef* and *Hell's Kitchen*, which often feature nouvelle cuisine-inspired dishes, and they wildly approve of presentation, health, freshness, light sauces, and new techniques, when gay hearts head out for a memorable dinner with friends, a spouse, or a first date, nouvelle cuisine becomes *not-enough* cuisine.

Sure the plate looks like a Picasso. The colors are dazzling. The presentation flawless. The taste simply orgasmic. But when the cube of meat, single pea, and lone carrot disappear in three bites and a gay heart finds himself licking the plate clean like a hungry dog, his tummy loudly roaring, "Is that it? Can't we order another round?" then all is not right in the foodie world. With the cost of nouvelle cuisine being sometimes higher than the average car payment, a second round is not likely. However, on the way home, a secretive stop at the golden arches or Taco Hell is likely to occur just to console the hungry gay heart.

IMPROPER USAGE OF UGGS

The popularity of ultra-comfy Uggs has caused a rash of fashion nightmares, blinding the eyes of gay hearts everywhere and causing them to weep like a sheep being shaved. Ugg wearers have taken to traipsing around in Uggs 24/7 all year round—even in 100 degree heat. The insanity of wearing sheepskin boots everywhere with everything has caused weepy gay hearts to issue this mandate . . .

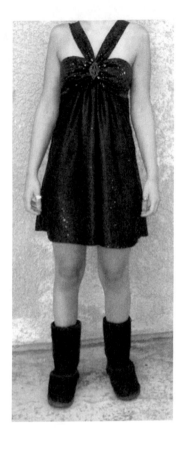

10 Ways Uggs Should Never Be Worn

1. With sweat pants tucked inside
2. With a dress
3. With sweatpants tucked inside and a dress over top
4. With short shorts (or any shorts)
5. With tights and short shorts
6. With bathing suits
7. While at the gym
8. While at the beach
9. While having sex
10. Any time after Memorial Day and before Labor Day

17 ♥ COUPLES WHO DRESS ALIKE

One of the best things about having a gay heart is celebrating individual style and not being afraid of self-expression. Unfortunately, as in the straight world, there are those gooey gay-heart couples who are so joined at the hip and lost into each other's worlds that they think it's fun to go out in public looking like the Gay Bobbsey Twins. This blatant display of "Look at us, aren't we cute" doesn't just make gay hearts weep, it makes them want to reach for a pair of scissors and cut away the revolting cuteness until there's nothing left but shreds of fabric on the ground and naked bodies running back into their Palm Beach condo. Single gay hearts are especially disturbed by couples dressing like twinsies—not because of any psychoanalytical observation, but because they secretly wish they could find their own soul mate to play matchy-match with and rub it in everyone's faces.

18 *JESUS CAMP* (THE MOVIE)

Gay hearts love a truly frightening horror movie. Give them the classic *Halloween*, the recent *Paranormal Activity*, and a marathon of *Saw* flicks for a good scare, but none will produce screams and pants-wetting like the documentary *Jesus Camp*. This terrifying and eye-opening film won tons of praise when it was released in 2006 and even garnered an Oscar nomination. (Thankfully, Al Gore's *Inconvenient Truth* won that year.)

For gay hearts, *Jesus Camp* has some of the most horrific moments ever captured on film. At a devout Christian summer camp, young children are being primed and brainwashed into becoming part of a hateful evangelical army aimed at delivering fundamentalist religious and political messages. Gay hearts shrink and quiver in their seats as they witness children being taught to hate Harry Potter, gay-sex-scandal pastor Ted Haggard bashing gays, and adults forcing children to stretch their hands out in prayer and worship a life-size cardboard cutout of George W. Bush. Truly, truly frightening cinema.

Five minutes into *Jesus Camp*, a gay heart will shake his head in disbelief and go, "Seriously, this isn't real . . ." This must be a mockumentary, the *Spinal Tap* of religious flicks, a really clever take on the Religious Right by spoof filmmaker extraordinaire Christopher Guest. Gay hearts will be waiting for Eugene Levy and Catherine O'Hara to appear, acting all zany and ridiculous, holding bibles. Once they discover that there's nothing funny about this horror camp and Parker Posey is nowhere to be found, the gay-heart weeping will begin, followed by guttural gay-heart screams.

Irony is not lost on *Jesus Camp*, either. For all its talk about sinners and nonbelievers on a rocketship to hell, it takes place at "Kids on Fire School of Ministry" near Devils Lake, North Dakota. For the Hollywood filmmaker gay heart, the references to hell and the devil present the perfect paradox: Are they secretly encouraging kids to become flamers?

19 BROKEN GAYDAR

When the gaydar goes down, the gay hearts weep. It's no fun hitting on someone who doesn't want what you have to offer, and gaydars are breaking down left and right these days. Gay hearts are finding it more and more difficult to tell if someone is gay or straight. Straight men are shopping too much at Nordstrom's and straight women are finding they like dressing down without makeup when they head to the grocery story. So it's an easy mistake for gay hearts to tap someone they should not be tapping. Broken gaydar = embarrassed weeping.

⟨20⟩ ASS CRACKS

The unexpected view of an ass crack will not only make the gay heart weep, but may possibly induce vomiting, depending on the size of the ass, how much crack is showing, and whether or not it's hairy, has pit marks, or reveals the tattooed head of a scary serpent peeking out. Many gay hearts will look away in disgust while others will whip out their cell phones, take a pic, and send it to all their friends. It's important to note that not all ass cracks horrify gay hearts. If the ass crack belonged to hottie ice skating gold medalist Evan Lycasek or bootylicious Beyoncé, there would definitely not being any weeping involved. Only awe.

21 RICHARD SIMMONS

Photo by Del Far

Flamboyant aerobics guru Richard Simmons makes gay hearts not only weep but cringe in disgust. Wearing his atrociously blinding crystal-covered tank tops and way too short dolphin shorts, Simmons has spent his lifetime acting gayer than a rainbow teddy bear, proclaiming all the while, "I'm not gay." With frizzy bad-perm hair, Simmons runs around screaming like a teenage girl, flipping wrists, doing high kicks, and brazenly flirting with men while milking a career that has turned him into a media whore as he lends his flaming persona to being violently joked about and ridiculed by late-night TV talk shows and corporate advertisers. Weeping gay hearts would like to say one thing to "not gay" Richie and his awful queenie image: Isn't it time to retire? Possibly find a nice woman and settle down? Your nauseating mockery of stereotypical gay men makes us weep with repulsion. Please, for the love of Nathan Lane in *Birdcage*, just stop.

22 MISSING THE OSCARS

Known as the Gay Super Bowl, the biggest night of the year for many gay hearts (except possibly Halloween) is the night Academy Awards are handed out. It doesn't matter one iota that a large percentage of gay hearts have not seen all of the nominated performances and films—watching the Oscars is all about Hollywood glamour and catching glimpses of favorite super-gays and gay-lovin' straight people. To celebrate the ten hours of TV viewing, Oscar parties are thrown! Gay-heart guests bring food dishes that must represent the Best Picture nominees, nominee lists are handed out with prizes given at the end of the night to those who get the most winners correct, and partygoers enjoy huge laughs about red carpet fashions from snarky gay hearts delivering memorable quips like "She looks like she bought a 50-percent-off shower curtain at Bed Bath & Beyond and attached it to her body with a glue gun! Somebody call a plumber!"

Missing the Oscars because of work, illness, a nephew's bar mitzvah, or a random power outage will undoubtedly leave a gay heart weeping melodramatically. Even though he knows he can watch the Oscars online, it's just not the same as experiencing it live. The luster and excitement are gone and gay hearts won't be excited about the Oscars again for another year.

CROCHETED ACCESSORIES

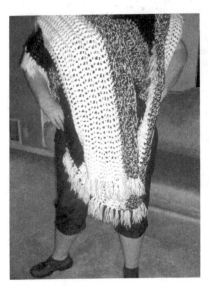

While knitting enjoys a comeback as a fun hobby that many gay hearts partake in, wearing crocheted accessories like hats, vests, and scarves is retro fashion fugliness that makes gay hearts weep tears of sparkle yarn. For decades all across the globe, drawers and closets have collected all kinds of nasty kaleidoscopic crocheted items made by grandmas, bored housewives, or friends caught up in the knitting craze. And that is where gay hearts say crocheted items should stay: in drawers and closets as keepsakes; locked up and out of sight from a gay heart's view. Crocheted blankets are the only exception; even something so awful as a purple and green afghan can be used for a cold winter night as long as it's returned to the plastic bin in the garage the next morning. People who continue to wear crocheted accessories out in public to the mall or grocery store should do so with caution. If spotted by a weeping gay heart who has been visually assaulted by whatever flower-panel, mohair-yarn monstrosity the crochet-wearer is flaunting, the gay heart will find a loose thread, grab hold of it, and run down the street until said item is a pile of string and no longer making them weep.

24 BAD KISSERS

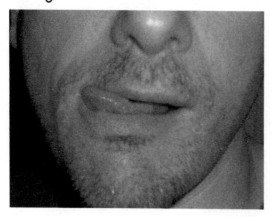

When it comes to kissing, gay hearts want the silver screen experience. They want a magical, stratospheric-swooning kiss that will make them feel like Jake Gyllenhaal and Heath Ledger in *Brokeback Mountain*, Susan Sarandon and Catherine Deneuve in *The Hunger*, or Scarlett finally giving in to Rhett in *Gone with the Wind*. But when someone whose mouth is open as wide as a loading dock comes at a gay heart, and it looks like he is about to be eaten instead of kissed, all he can do is turn away in weepy horror.

There are many kinds of Bad Kissers: Face Lickers, who want to stick their tongues up nostrils; Zombie Kissers, who want to eat face with their teeth; Driller Kissers, who want to shove their tongue down a throat like a medical probe; and Cement Kissers, whose shuttered tight lips leads one to believe they have no interest in being kissed in the first place!

Bad kissers make a gay heart weep, but also tempt them to be brutally honest by telling lousy smoochers that they need to go to kissing school or their kissing days are numbered.

Fortunately, the gay heart has recommendations for bad kissers to help improve their skills: watch a bunch of romance or porn movies, or, better yet, recruit the next-door neighbor for some real-time training.

25 EXPENSIVE DRINKS

It's been said, but it bears repeating: Gay hearts love to drink! What they don't love is paying $10 for a watered-down martini in a Dixie cup.

Expensive drinks = fewer drinks = lots of weeping.

THE SNUGGIE BLANKET

A blanket designed in the exact same shape as a hospital gown? Gay hearts weep at the very sight of a Snuggie blanket! They don't understand why millions of these backward robes have been sold in such awful colors and prints and why on earth anyone would want to sit on their couch looking like a suburban monk.

For cold winter nights, most gay hearts prefer curling up in a cozy afghan or down comforter. However, there are a select few who secretly own Snuggies for themselves and their poor unwilling dogs. These gay hearts are the same ones who secretly wear Crocs. Crocs and the Snuggie will be typically worn together, but only inside their homes with the shades drawn.

27 NICHOLAS SPARKS BOOKS AND MOVIES

Although gay hearts have never read any of his books, they weep over Nicholas Sparks's sappy straight romance novels because they are forced to view portions of his terribly cliché love stories as irritating TV commercials, films at theater complexes (when more gay-heart happy fare like *Sex in the City* sells out and there's nothing to see), or on late night cable TV (when they accidentally land on a random channel and stay there because of Richard Gere's charisma or Channing Tatum's body).

For the love of Michael Thomas Ford and Rita Mae Brown, gay hearts wish Sparks would go into retirement because he has more money than John Grisham and Janet Evanovich combined. Does the world really need another one of his sleepy yarns that will end up on the silver screen in five minutes assaulting gay-heart eyeballs with the likes of Mandy Moore and Miley Cyrus? Sparks has said in interviews that he could never write about gay love and this makes gay hearts sigh with relief, because if he did do a gay *Notebook*, it would probably be so lousy and boring they wouldn't just weep, they'd drop to the floor and melodramatically bawl. Just like one of his characters.

With the exception of Lady Gaga Ga's tour bus and the big pink party bus in the movie *Priscilla, Queen of the Desert*, gay hearts weep and shudder over having to ride in a bus. They do not enjoy being smashed inside of a stifling, uncomfortable, fashionless, stinky, and sometimes filthy tin box on wheels with throngs of sweaty straight people, unpredictable crazies, and screaming rug rats. And God forbid a gay heart has to travel on a Greyhound type of bus for any lengthy period of time. The actual thought of being on a fifteen-hour ride from one state to another without alcohol makes them want to jump out while it's still moving and hitchhike. The only kind of bus-like vehicle that gay hearts don't mind getting aboard, and actually enjoy, is the Disneyland Tram because they know it's a short ride and it's taking them to the happiest place on earth.

♡ 29 BAD WINE

Not all gay hearts are wine connoisseurs, but they savor the taste of delicious wine—expensive or cheap. Serving a gay heart novelty vino with funny names from pretty designer bottles filled with shitty and low-grade wine that tastes like fermented monkey sweat will not only leave them weeping, but force the gay heart to go behind the host's back and deviously find a place to rid himself of the foul beverage—like the terra cotta pot holding the giant plastic palm.

Never serve a gay heart any of these wines:

- Boone's Farm
- Ed Hardy
- Sparkling Cold Duck
- Charles Shaw (aka 2 Buck Chuck)
- Bitch
- Martini & Rossi Asti Spumante
- Blue Nun
- V. Sattui
- Franzia

30 A WII FIT COLLECTING DUST

Unbeknownst to many straight people, gay hearts are huge gamers. They love their Wii, Xbox, PlayStation 3, Nintendo DS, and Guitar Hero, and most own them all because they love having their coordination skills randomly tested and can't get enough play time from the unique games that each unit has to offer.

However, many gay hearts weep with buyer's remorse after spending hundreds of dollars on the Wii Fit and all its accessories: a Wii balance board, Wii yoga mat, Wii ankle and wrist weights, Wii dumbbells, Wii pushup bar, Wii step platform, Wii snow/skateboard, and of course a Wii exercise kit that includes stuff like Wii head and wrist bands, Wii exercise speedometer, Wii resistance bands, Wii socks, and a nifty Wii water bottle. When gay hearts go in, they go in big and get it all. Unfortunately, when gay hearts find themselves in front of the TV, ready for some gaming action, and a choice has to be made between doing Wii Fit's Pilates with Daisy Fuentes or having a rock show with Guitar Hero's Aerosmith, the loser is obvious. And there the Wii Fit console will sit: in a dark corner, collecting dust, and possibly holding a potted plant.

NO INTERNET ACCESS

Not being able to get online will not only make gay hearts weep, it will send them into a wild, manic, sweaty, shaking panic that's way worse than anything a strung-out heroin addict would show after not being able to get a fix for a week. Jonesing for Internet access could cause mild-mannered gay hearts to do crazy, unpredictable things that they never in a million years would do, like ask total strangers at the airport if they can borrow their laptop or beg a tween at the grocery store to let them use their iPhone because they can't get service. Gay hearts need their Internet. Ten minutes without e-mail, Facebook, Twitter, YouTube, World of Warcraft, TMZ, Amazon, After Elton/After Ellen, and the Huffington Post would be nothing short of Armageddon.

SIDEWAYS TRUCKER HATS

Gay hearts weep for the morons (mostly straights) who think it's cool and hip to wear any kind of baseball cap with the brim to the side like someone just smacked them in the face with a two-by-four. Gay hearts weep not just because this looks supremely idiotic and pathetic, but because an idiot strutting around with his cap to the side acting like he's the shit in front of everyone is nothing more than a huge douchebag.

33 ♡ MANOREXIA

Manorexia has taken the younger gay community by storm, and gay hearts weep for the scrawny skin-and-bones younger gay hearts who look like they are on an emo hunger strike or have spent a lot of time working out their throat muscles at the toilet. When gay hearts see a fellow gay heart stricken with manorexia, they want to kidnap him (there would not be much of a struggle because manorexic gay hearts are so frail they can barely put on their women's jeans) and take him to a Jewish mother's house, where she will force-feed the manorexic gay heart until he's put some weight back on. Many gay-heart manorexics are fashion models and live off a diet of heavy alcohol, Monster energy drinks, and bags of Funyuns. It's not clear how manorexia started, but studies have shown that those afflicted with it only think about food and pass out. It doesn't help that many of them don't know how to cook. This also makes gay hearts weep because not caring about food or not being able to cook reminds them of straight men.

³⁴ INSTANT COFFEE

As bleary-eyed gay hearts stumble out of bed, for many the first business of the day is to get some caffeine pumping through their veins. Gay hearts will go to any extreme to get the coffee they love—driving to a coffee shop a block away, running to Whole Foods to get that perfect organic bean, or making a delicious soy latte with their own home espresso machine. But if they are forced to drink any kind of freeze-dried coffee that quickly dissolves in water with a quick stir like Tang, gay hearts will weep in disgust. To them, all instant coffee is putrid coffee-flavored water designed to be palatable to the masses with obviously broken taste buds. At hotels and on airplanes, gay hearts will avoid instant coffee as if it's sewer water, choosing to drink a Coke, an energy drink, or martini instead.

However, if a gay heart finds himself spending the weekend with the grandparents and grandpa Vic is right there in the morning all bright-eyed and bushy-tailed, holding out a fresh cup of his famous Folgers instant, it's a lot harder to say, "Sorry, gramps, I don't drink that radiation shit." This gay heart loves his grandpa and will take a few weeping sips to make him happy before dumping it in the sink when grandpa isn't looking, and then will suddenly announce he needs to run to the store for allergy medicine (which he finds at Starbucks). For gay hearts it has to be real coffee or no coffee at all.

KNOCK-OFF PORN

Gay hearts weep when porno filmmakers crank out scary sex parodies of their beloved Hollywood films. Gay hearts weep over these lame knockoffs because when they want to see some hot sweaty action to get them all worked up, just looking at the cover of *Golden Girls, A Triple MILF Parody*, which mocks their beloved TV show with porn stars wearing old lady wigs, will make the fire in their loins weep out and die.

It's important to know that there are some gay hearts who weep not because of porno films knocking off Hollywood, but because they love watching them for laughs and none of these titles are available on Netflix so they will have to resort to watching crappy gay coming-out comedies.

LAME KNOCKOFF
GAY PORN TITLES

Twinklight
Raiders of the Lost Arse
Black Whore Down
The Little Sperm-maid
Lord of the Cock Rings—The Two Ta-Ta's
The Bitches of Madison County
Mr. Smith Does Washington
One Came Over the Cuckoo's Nest
The Sexorcist
Shitty Shitty Bang Bang
Star Whores—The Empire Gets It in the Ass
Star Whores—Revenge of the Clit
Star Whores—A New Ho
Bed Knobs and Brown Dicks
Sex Trek II
Shaving Ryan's Privates
Four Crossdressers and a Sexchange
The Slutty Professor
Fantastic Foursome
Charley Takes It in the Chocolate Factory
The Da Vinci Load
Jurassic Cock
Ferris Bueller's Gay Boff
Edward Dildo Hands
The Queer Hunter
12 Naked Men
Boner and Clyde
E.T. The Extra-Testicle

PEOPLE WHO CAN'T PARK

When gay hearts are weeping because there is no valet service and they are driving around in circles at the mall searching frantically for parking before the movie starts, they weep even harder when they see a car parked over the lines taking up two spaces. Some gay hearts will grumble and sigh while continuing to drive around for another half hour, while others will take a more hands-on approach and do one of the following:

1. Try and squeeze in the space making it difficult for the other driver to get into their car. (This is only done if the gay heart has a shitty car and they don't care if it gets dinged.)
2. Surround the poorly parked vehicle with as many shopping carts as possible.
3. Leave a nasty note that says something like: "Nice parking job ass bag! I did something to your car and I'm not going to tell you what it is." (Most gay hearts would never vandalize an illegally parked car, but knowing the driver has to look over their vehicle with a magnifying glass for an hour makes their gay heart fill with warm joy.)
4. Toilet paper the selfishly parked car till it looks like a giant mummy.

5. Park in a way that blocks them in.
6. Leave a note that says: "Dear Entitled Mercedes Driver, You look rich, so why don't you go buy yourself some parking lessons, or better yet, why not STOP driving all together and hire a driver. Then we Honda drivers won't have to deal with your selfishness and be tempted to egg your SL."

OVERUSING "OMG"

Like everyone else in America, gay hearts can't stop saying or texting "OMG" (oh my god) and they weep because their uncontrollable behavior has turned them into OMG addicts and they can't stop saying OMG no matter what emotion they are having:

"OMG did you see what she was wearing?"
"OMG is that really the price on those Marc Jacobs boots?"
"OMG do you smell the grease coming from that burger joint?"
"OMG thank you SOOO much, I always wanted Prada sunglasses."
"OMG you are so sweet I want to kiss you!"
"Oh. My. God. I can't believe the size of that thing!"

Although it may be hard to believe, there are a few brave gay hearts who have realized their communication skills have dwindled and they are willing to rehabilitate their OMG usage. So they have formed support groups like "No More OMG" or "The Three Letters That Must Not Be Spoken or Texted." At these meetings gay hearts work with English teachers on replacing OMG with actual sentences that have more than three little words. The only problem with these groups is that once a gay heart stops saying OMG they replace it with WTF? Then it's only a matter of minutes before there are texting them together.

38 TWITTER DIARRHEA

Although OMG-spouting gay hearts dig Twitter and can be found tweeting daily and following their favorite super-gays and gay-lovin' celebrities, they tweet-weep over the condition known as twitterrhea. Much like diarrhea, twitterrhea is a barrage of unstoppable tweets containing unimportant stupid shit often full of incomplete sentences and abbreviations that make no sense:

1. "hey everybody sitting on the couch tweeting!"
2. "my cat ginger is watching me tweet!"
3. "look at me! I'm on a toilet tweeting! lol"
4. "IOW twitterpated! TTYS"

When gay hearts encounter twitterrhea they immediately unfollow unless it belongs to Britney Spears, Courtney Love, or Kathy Griffin (there are some people whose twitterrhea is just too entertaining to pass up).

Gay hearts would also like to remind everyone to be mindful of what you tweet about your friends, and always, always: Google before you tweet!

39 M. NIGHT SHYAMALAN MOVIES

Gay hearts weep cinematic tears every time they are tricked into going to a movie theater and shelling out fifteen bucks to see another shitty M. Night Shyamalan movie. Bamboozled by slick, mesmerizing previews and advertising that led them to believe his new movie will be the big summer blockbuster ride they can talk about with their friends, gay hearts end up flocking to his movies on opening weekend only to leave the theater wanting to slap themselves in the head while saying, "What was I thinking? All his movies suck!"

Well, maybe not all his movies. M. Night's first film, *The Sixth Sense*, wowed gay hearts with the engrossing performance of a little boy who could "see dead people." The follow-up was gay-heart favorite Bruce Willis in *Unbreakable*, which was not Unacceptable or Unwatchable, just boring, with another gimmicky twist at the end. Then came *Signs* with crazy Mel and previews that made gay hearts think it was going to be a scary *Close Encounters* or *Independence Day*. Not so. Gay hearts flocked to the theater for that ball of confusion and left scratching their heads while feeling sleepy.

What followed were horrible, weepy coma-inducing films that had tons of buzz and advertising making them look like must-see event films: *The Village*, *Lady in the Water*, *The Happening*, and *The Last Airbender*. Gay hearts would like M. Night to know they've had enough of his movies, and until he can come up with something worthy enough to justify the ever-increasing price of a movie ticket, they will be playing the wait-and-see game after opening weekend. No more cinematic trickery from you, Mr. M. If your next film does not live up to gay hearts' movie-going standards, they will withhold the weeping and wait to order it on Netflix so when it makes them confused and sleepy in the comfort of their own home, they can flip to something better on HBO.

40 ♥ SLOW PORN DOWNLOADS

Gay male hearts live for their porn, but when they want it, they want it NOW. Their horny gay hearts weep and go limp when the download becomes slower than an IRS office processing tax refunds.

41 STUPID GAY T-SHIRTS

While gay hearts weep at the sight of a stupid gay T-shirt and claim to "not be caught dead" wearing one in public, nearly all gay hearts have a favorite stupid gay T-shirt they wear to bed. Here are some of the very worst offenders:

- I love caulk
- Lesbian by birth, butch by choice
- There's some seaman on my shirt
- Amateur gynecologist
- Amateur proctologist
- Me so horny
- Pussy lover
- Hi, I'm a top
- Lezbot
- Sorry, my boyfriend's in town
- It's not gonna lick itself
- I left the straight back in the closet
- I only look straight
- Fruits are people too
- Everyone always loves a lesbian
- Everyone always loves a gay boy
- My roommate is gay
- Gaysians do it best
- Nobody knows I'm gay
- My bush is pro choice
- Dolphins are just gay sharks
- Dykeville
- Gayborhood
- Vagitarian
- Butt Pirate

42 CHUBBY PEOPLE IN TIGHT CLOTHES

One thing that will set a gay heart off into weeping is the sudden sight of a marshmallow-like creature revealing its flabby spare tire popping out from ill-fitting clothes that look on the verge of ripping at any second. Weeping gay hearts don't understand why this person would walk around like this in front of God and everyone and think it's okay. If only there was an app to make Carson Kressley magically appear to correct the fashion emergency.

43 FUGLY DESIGNER CLOTHES

Gay hearts weep when their favorite designers, many of them also gay, design something so heinously awful they wouldn't give it to their worst enemy. Gay hearts also weep when they see straight people in fugly designer clothes thinking they are fashionistas, parading around like they are walking down a red carpet flooded with paparazzi. To gay hearts these fashion disasters look more like they're wearing secondhand store rejects. Gay hearts want to drop to their knees and weep, "Why Michael Kors, why? You are a judge on *Project Runway* and you constantly complain about things looking 'home sewn'! How could you ever let that hideous bathrobe-looking dress escape from your design studio?"

JUSTIN BIEBER

Photo by Kevin Aranibar, NYC

Gay hearts weep at the very sight or mention of Justin Bieber. While many gay heart girls are replicating his eyeball-stabbing hair style (and there's even a website for it called LesbiansWho LookLikeJustinBieber.com), gay heart boys are yawning, saying they want to see what happens in ten years. If they had any advice to give young Justin, it would be to stop making YouTube videos of himself blow drying his hair.

45 ♡ HAT VIOLATIONS

There is only one person on the planet gay hearts feel can wear a horrible hat and not cause weepiness, and that's Lady Gaga! While creating hat violations just about every day, only Gaga can pull off wearing a jaw-dropping monstrosity and still make it look like high fashion. When Gaga bravely sports a helmet-shaped chapeau with a reindeer antler sticking out from the top at a movie premier, they know she's not taking herself seriously. However, the rest of the world should use extreme caution when deciding to put any of these frightening creations on their head:

- Pimp hats with feathers
- Crocheted sun hats with floral panels
- Giant ear-flap fur hats
- Knit caps worn in the middle of summer
- Hawaiian-print bucket hats
- Knit caps accented with peacock feathers and jewels
- Trucker hats with stupid phrases
- Gaudy over-decorated church hats
- Motorcycle helmets worn indoors
- Hat and wig combos
- Floppy oversized sun hats
- Cable-knit bonnets
- Du-rags
- Beer helmets

46 OLD BARS THAT SMELL LIKE PISS

Gay hearts love going out to bars, especially trendy clubs with current dance music, amazing atmospheres, and bars with hotties serving up exotic drinks. Therefore it comes as no surprise that when gay hearts are forced to hang out in an old dive bar that smells like piss, they will weep! Although the less-than-pleasant surroundings of foul odors and wretched rundown decor cause them to bawl like they were Paris Hilton shopping at TJ Maxx, gay hearts love their liquor so much that they don't actually mind if they land in a dive bar. Instead of leaving, they just start drinking. Heavily. Within no time the old bar that smells like piss doesn't seem so old and pissy any more—it feels like home, as nice as any overpriced haunt in a trendy part of town. Cheers!

47 BAGGY FLEECE SWEATSUITS

A sure-fire way to make a gay heart weep is to give them a baggy fleece sweatsuit as a present. It doesn't matter how amazing the color is or what city is airbrushed across the front or how comfy they might feel while spending the day being a couch potato, gay hearts shudder at the mere sight of the elastic-waist fleece pants with ribbed cuffs. They won't even try to return it to the store. Instead they'll immediately take the revolting sweats outside to their back yard, throw them in the barbeque pit, douse them with fluid, and light them on fire. (Of course more responsible gay hearts would actually donate their heinous sweatsuit gift to a homeless person—as long as the homeless person lives in a neighborhood far away because gay hearts would not want to see the nasty tracksuit walking down any of their streets.)

AS SEEN ON TV PRODUCTS

May gay hearts love entertaining themselves late at night watching ridiculously awful, but often hilarious infomercials for As Seen on TV products. Who didn't laugh every time the spry little old lady in bed put her hands together to clap the lights off using The Clapper? Or watching sexual-harassment-lawsuit-waiting-to-happen Tony Little go to town like a redneck chasing a beer on The Gazelle. Or how about Tiddy Bear, the mini stuffed bear that slips over a seatbelt in your car and claims to create comfort while looking like it's copping a feel. From Chia Pets to Spray-on Hair, As Seen on TV products have taken over the world with the little red TV logo stamp prominently displayed on every package. Like everyone else, gay hearts have found themselves pulling out their credit cards, only to weep later on when they have a closet or drawer full of these useless products that at one time promised to make life easier. Gay hearts also weep over As Seen on TV products because every year when the holidays roll around, they know they'll receive no fewer than three of them as gifts, which they will immediately re-gift. However if anyone gives them The Comfort Wipe (a curved plastic stick that holds toilet paper for ass-wiping) there's a good chance the gift-giver might just get hit with it.

THE WEEPIEST AS SEEN ON TV PRODUCTS

The Neckline Slimmer
Foot Aligner Socks
Ronco Pocket Fisherman
The Original Magic Bullet Express Blender
Pant Stretcher
Odor Assassin
Couch Coaster
Tater Mitts
Button Extender
Bumpits
Smokeless Ashtray
The Bedazzler
Head On
Sham Wow
The Flowbee Vacuum Haircut System
My Lil' Reminder
Meatball Magic
Self-tanning Wipes
6-Second Abs

PEOPLE WHO WANT TO POP OTHER PEOPLE'S ZITS

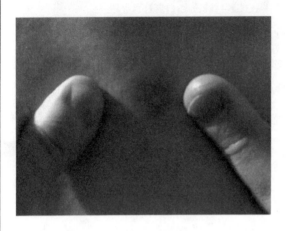

If a gay heart hears the sentence "Oh my God, you have a zit, please let me pop it!" and sees two index fingers coming toward them like scalpels, he will not only weep but gag with disgust while threatening to take out a zit-protecting restraining order. Zit poppers freak gay hearts out. Extremely attentive to their own skin, they believe that when and where a zit gets popped and who does the popping is an extremely personal issue and should be left up to the zit's owner. People who suddenly want to pop other people's zits at random in public places—say, at a skating rink—really should learn to contain their disturbing gross behavior. If these zit poppers are so deliriously desperate to pop something, they should head on over to Office Depot and buy a roll of bubble wrap. Then they can pop to their heart's content, instead of going after some poor gay heart's weeping face.

CRAIGSLIST LIARS

No matter what it is, when a gay heart needs to buy something he can't find, sell something he wants to get rid of, or meet the love of his life, Craigslist is a bookmarked favorite. Like the rest of America, Craigslist has become gay hearts' connection to concert tickets, job networking, apartments, cars, and, yes, most notably the place to find a hookup for gay heart boys. The weeping begins when they encounter people who lie on Cragislist. They lie about how good the concert seats are, or don't say that the apartment is a closet instead of a room, or won't admit to the true condition of a 1997 Mazda Protegé. And there are those Craigslist Liars who even fib about themselves; saying they look like Taylor Lautner and they're well-endowed, when in reality they look like Gilbert Gottfried and have a micro penis. Weeping gay hearts who love going on Craigslist and using it for everything, would like everyone to please have some dignity and post responsibly. It's just not nice or good karma to lie and say the hundred dollar air pump is brand new in the box and never used, and what they're selling is used and broken as seen here.

51 NOT OWNING AN IPHONE

The very few gay hearts who don't own an iPhone definitely weep because they are without the almighty magical instrument treasured by so many. With gay hearts being big fans of anything Apple—they all own iPods and many are Mac users—to them not having an iPhone is like living out in the Old West without a shotgun. Even those gay hearts who are Blackberry users have dumped their crackberry ball-scrolling for the easy iPhone life of touch-screen. Gay hearts love the nifty features iPhone has, like landscape keyboard for bigger fingers, shaking the phone to undo typing, iPhone chat, video calling, instant YouTube access, and the Find My iPhone tracker for when they've lost their phone (usually left at a hookup's house). Gay hearts have also gone completely iPhone app crazy and cannot get enough of them. They use apps for everything: help with grocery lists, cooking, traveling, finding hookups, and even testing their French-kissing skills! A gay heart without an iPhone is like Don Draper without a whiskey or cigarette in hand (or a woman, depending on how you want to look at it).

♡ 52 HIPSTERS

KEEP OFF HIPSTERS

Photo by Infrogmation of New Orleans

Whenever gay hearts notice an area is being infiltrated by "hipsters" they weep to keep from gagging. To gay hearts, hipsters are part of an annoying pack, basically a bunch of skinny, too-cool-for-school straight people believing they are trendsetters, wearing alternative new fashions, hitting the least-known new bars, listening to the latest music (regardless of whether it's actually any good), and seeing all the new independent films (regardless of whether they're any good). In reality, these so-called hipsters are regurgitating everything gay hearts did fifteen minutes ago—just with a lot more apathy and much less panache. Gay hearts wouldn't weep as much if these hipster copycats would go find their own damn style.

CAPRI PANTS

Gay hearts weep for the hideousness of Capri pants. They weep because no one—man, woman, child, dog, or cat—should have to wear pants that make them look like they outgrew their old clothes and can't afford to buy new ones. Weeping gay hearts would like to see all these ready-for-the-flood-almost-shorts-but-not-quite Capri pants dumped into an active volcano. Capri pants should be outlawed. Call your congressman or woman! Don't stand for the fashion industry producing Capri pants and telling everyone they look good in them!

54 DOGS COSTUMES

Gay hearts' dogs are often attired in designer wear. Nothing but the best for their pooches: Juicy Couture shirts, Burberry sweaters, and Gucci coats. Outerwear is a doggie must during the chilly cold months of winter, but when gay hearts see dogs dressed in ridiculous, silly costumes and clothes for no apparent reason other than to amuse owners who thinks it's cute to show off their precious Fluffy or Fido, gay hearts weep for their canine friends.

Just look at the little French bulldog pictured here. Does she look like she wants to be dressed up like a bumblebee for the 4th of July family picnic? No, she does not. If it's not Halloween or some special doggie masquerade ball (where she is showered with doggie treats), gay hearts say: Don't humiliate your dogs with stupid costumes. Inside they are weeping (while plotting a way to tear off the unbearable getup).

55 HAVING TO TRAP OR KILL A ROACH OR MOUSE

Even the butchest gay-heart girls and the buffest gay-heart boys get wimpy—and weepy—when it comes to encounters with unwanted critters in their castles. The sight of a king-size roach or unruly rodent scurrying across the floor will make them scream like Richard Simmons (well, hopefully not *quite* like that). If gay hearts do not have the proper traps or pesticides to rid their pads of these pesky creatures, they look for any kind of protection they can find, like trying to suck them up with the vacuum cleaner or squash them with the cheap IKEA floor lamp, or throwing David Sedaris books, empty beer bottles, and ABBA CDs until the giant black insect is dead. If none of these tricks work, a terrified gay heart will resort to grabbing the first thing under the kitchen sink, like a can of Glade air freshener which they will hastily seize, aim, and fire until the can is empty or the bug stops moving. Gay hearts don't enjoy killing God's creatures, but large crawling things are creepy *and* weepy.

♡ 56 BAD TIPPERS

Gay hearts are the best tippers in the world. This is most likely due to the fact that so many of them make a living as waiters and waitresses. Having themselves been stiffed and undercompensated (usually by straight people) for service, gay hearts take bad tipping personally and refuse to stand by and allow it to happen. If a gay heart is dining with a big group of friends and the tip is not adequate, they will always step up and fork over the extra bucks to make sure their server has been adequately compensated. However, even as gay hearts loathe bad tippers, they loathe bad service even more. As quickly as they reward with a 30 percent tip for outstanding service, they won't think twice about dropping two pennies on the table if the service is crap.

RIDICULOUS FETISHES

Most gay hearts are respectful of the limitless fetishes that both gay-heart girls and gay-heart boys love to take part in. Some naughty leather, a little fun roleplay, a cop costume, some sexy underwear, an attraction to toes, a love for earlobes— whatever the fetish, gay hearts are happy to live and let live, as everyone has his or her own unique desires. However when gay hearts see strange sexual fare like people rubbing their naked bodies on balloons to get off, someone wanting to be strangled before they orgasm, or a grown man humping a large pink teddy bear on a bed surrounded by other terrified stuffed animals, it pretty much freaks them out and the fetish weeping begins—along with an offer of referral to a really good therapist.

WEEPIEST FETISHES

- Disney character roleplay
- Attraction to appliances
- Sex with balloons
- Doing naughty things to a stuffed plush bunny
- Doing naughty things in a plush bunny suit
- Rubber body suits completely covering the face and head
- Falconry
- Anything involving a gerbil
- Diapers
- Blue body paint
- Harry Potter costumes

58 HAVING TO GET UP BEFORE 9 IN THE MORNING

Having to get up early—any time before 9 A.M.—will make gay hearts weep. Some will weep for about ten seconds before they roll back over after the five-second decision to keep sleeping and start their day late. Other gay hearts may not have that luxury and have to get up at 6 or 7 A.M. They do this, of course, weeping all the way, to the shower, the closet, and the car. The weeping over having to get up early does not stop until large amounts of coffee are consumed and the weeping is replaced with caffeine jitters, which eventually makes them forget about having to get up at the crack of dawn. Gay hearts weeping over early mornings has always been part of their culture—it's why they love brunch (as opposed to breakfast), shopping the mall, or going to a matinee. It's the idea that nothing is going on till after 10 anyway. Why get up? Gay-heart beauty rest is needed.

59 TAKING A BAD PICTURE

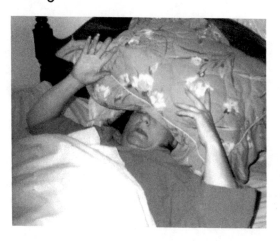

Gay hearts weep tears of embarrassment when they discover they've taken a bad photo. With Facebook being the go-to place to see photos from the beer bust BBQ, a friend's wild birthday party, or last Saturday night's bar-hopping adventure, it makes photo weeping even more intense because rarely is anyone given the opportunity to nix or Photoshop a really shitty picture of themselves. Said photo usually gets posted without warning to the gay heart's wall, and by the time he sees himself looking like he had gained fifty pounds, partied with Ron Wood, and contracted a case of malaria, all of his 500 friends have also seen the photo. The damage has been done and the gay heart weeps while hitting the delete button.

WEEPIEST PHOTO POSES

- Taking a picture of oneself in the mirror with the camera visible
- Grabbing the chin with one hand in a creepy Sherlock Holmes pervert way
- Hands curled into cat claws with lips in snarl
- Holding hand up to open mouth in fake surprise expression
- Hands together in prayer pose placed at the side of the head as if ready for beddy-bye

MORE WEEPIEST PHOTO POSES

- Blowing a kiss like you're freakin' Marilyn Monroe
- Fists clenched in fisti-cuffs fighting stance (with someone or at the camera)
- Making the peace sign (with one or both hands)
- Getting two or more people in a group to do their version of kissy face

BREAD MAKES YOU FAT

Gay hearts everywhere weep when they come to the realization that bread makes them fat. Of course, this doesn't stop them from eating bread, it just makes them weep bitter buttery tears while they work through the bakery fresh-from-the-oven cinnamon raisin loaf before moving onto croissants and sourdough rolls.

61 FIST-BUMPING

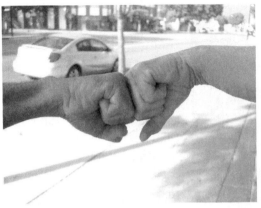

Whenever straight men hold out a fist for a gay heart boy to bump, he pulls out his own fist and follows through with the knuckle clash, all the while weeping inside at how ridiculously dorky he looks and feels. For this very reason, you will never see gay hearts doing fist bumps with each other. Although fist-bumping looks like it began in a high school locker room with a football coach, there has been speculation that it may have started in the gay community. But these rumors were undoubtedly started by clueless straight people. Gay hearts have no need for such a weepy, macho, impersonal greeting. They are too busy kissing and hugging everyone.

62 VENETIAN BLIND SUNGLASSES

Gay hearts weep over one of the most hideous accessories ever designed in fashion history: venetian blind sunglasses. Also known as Shudder Shades, gay hearts don't understand why anyone would want to wear robotic-looking glasses that make you feel like you are peeking out the window at someone while resembling a distant humanoid cousin to C-3PO from *Star Wars*.

Venetian blind sunglasses were hot in the '80s and gay hearts were hoping that's where they'd stay—until their gay hearts began instantly weeping when singer Kanye West brought them back from oblivion for his video *Stronger* (which is a song that makes many gay hearts happy). While the glasses Kanye wore on stage and in his video fit the theme he was after and got the updated name of Grill Glasses, gay hearts were not fooled into thinking shutter blinds were hot eyewear again. Any gay heart will tell you the coolest sunglasses ever of the '80s were Ray-Ban's Wayfarer. No weeping there. Only gay heart style.

SIGNING UP FOR A GYM AND NEVER USING IT

Gay hearts weep over signing up for a gym and never using it. Dreaming of acquiring a body like Ryan Reynolds, many gay-heart boys will go through the sign-up motions, pay membership-joining fees, have the monthly fee deducted from their debit card, and in some cases hire a trainer. While some will end up looking like Spartan Gerard Butler in the movie *300*, others will lose interest several weeks later and give their trainers excuses why they can't work out that usually involve their dog getting sick and needing to be rushed to the vet or their having to go out of town for three weeks. For many gay hearts, when it comes to the choice of hitting the gym or the martini bar for happy hour, the cosmo always trumps a dumbbell.

64 TACKY CAR ACCESSORIES

Whenever gay hearts see or are forced to ride in a car filled with tacky car accessories they get freaked-out-weepy. The cause: scary dashboard bobble heads, fluffy dice, pictures of Jesus, hideous seat covers, nodding ultra-suede dogs and cats, strange and stinky air-fresheners, and stuffed animals scattered everywhere. Truth be told, there are many gay hearts who love to decorate their cars with similar items; however, these tacky car accessories will be themed in rainbows, photos of half-naked men, and Betty Page trinkets. But nothing makes a gay heart weep and cringe more than having to get into a filthy, ashtray-smelling car full of food crumbs, trash, and odd items that never made it back into the house. The smiling bobble head hula dancer on the dashboard might be a little frightening, but it's nothing compared to feeling they'll need to be sanitized and hosed down by the time they get to their destination.

FASHION FAILURES

Gay hearts weep like Anna Wintour when they are randomly blinded by any stranger walking down the street sporting ghastly fashion mistakes. Although many gay male hearts are perpetrators of fashion failures daily by overusing bright designer colors that make them look like clowns from Cirque Du Soleil, they are all acutely aware of the fashion sin captured in the photo here: Camouflage pleated skirt with motorcycle boots and a structured handbag. This person needs to be stripped and sent to the TLC show *What Not To Wear.* Let Stacy London and Clinton Kelly deal with them.

ALL-TIME WEEPIEST FASHION FAUX PAS

Guys wearing girls' pants
Bell bottoms and platforms
High-waist jeans
Velour sweatsuits
Chinese slippers
Leg warmers
Shoulder pads
Crop tops
Pants with writing on the ass
Ponchos
Fanny packs
Parachute pants
Grillz
Shell tracksuits

Headbands

Crocs

Hawaiian shirts

Anything tie-dyed

Popped collars

Puffy sleeves

Skinny jeans

Print shirts with matching ties

66 NO STARBUCKS WITHIN WALKING DISTANCE

Many Americans have become inherently lazy with their morning coffee, forfeiting the use of their state-of-the-art coffeemakers for a trip to the nearest coffee house selling fancy $5 lattes. And coffee connoisseur gay hearts are no different! They will get out of bed half asleep, throw clothes on, stumble out the door (walking past the kitchen and the dusty Krups), and walk a block wiping sleep from their eyes to go stand in line at Starbucks, Coffee Bean, or any other decent coffee house. Price is no object for gay hearts with the wish to get coffee in hand as easily as possible so they can get their brain functioning and body moving! They also don't want to worry about cleaning the coffee maker and prepping it for the next day. It's just too much work! Who has the time?

If gay hearts find themselves in a situation where there is no Starbucks, Coffee Bean, or any other decent coffee house within a five minute walk, there will be plenty of weeping, followed by a grouchy caffeine meltdown and a frantic search for car keys so they can drive to the nearest java joint five miles away. Gay hearts love having a Starbucks across the street, even if they aren't really a Starbucks fan; it's not about the brand, it's about being able to get any fancy flavorful coffee with special ingredients like soy milk, whipped cream, chocolate syrup, and triple shots. Although it takes more effort to get dressed, leave the house, and walk across the street, gay hearts want the instant gratification of having their morning cup of Joe handed directly to them so they can begin sucking the coffee out, like it's an IV going right into their blood stream. A gay heart will never move into a neighborhood that does not have a respectable coffee outlet within two blocks of his home. The issue is not unlike a town without a Target, Trader Joe's, or Whole Foods; being able to buy a caramel macchiato double within minutes of their bedroom is a life choice that is non-negotiable for gay hearts who rely on a morning coffee fix.

JUNK ROOMS

Gay hearts weep over the secret place in their homes where they dump stuff they don't know what to do with. Homeowners call them junk rooms, and to many apartment dwellers they are known as junk closets and junk drawers. However, all three junk places can be found in some homes that are well on their way to becoming candidates for the *Hoarders* TV show.

When something is thought to be located in the so-called junk room, a feeling of dread is felt followed by a sigh, and then possibly a "Fuck, it's in the junk room." Then begins the long arduous task of maneuvering through the treacherous junk room to find the suddenly needed missing item, which is usually something stupid like an ugly southwestern-themed table vase given by friends that now has to be brought out because said friends are coming for dinner. Gay heart weeping follows as they stumble over broken exercise equipment, boxes of discarded photos and photo albums, plastic tubs full of Christmas and Halloween decorations, a badminton net, an old fish aquarium, boxes full of free stuff collected at gay pride parades, old broken lamps, beach chairs, and shopping bags full of who-knows-what.

Gay hearts weeping over their junky rooms, closets, and drawers constantly vow to get them cleaned up, especially after they've had to spend two hours rummaging through one to find their birth certificate. "This is a good rainy day project," they'll say, or "Come hell or high water, I'm cleaning this out on Sunday!" But for most it never happens, the rainy day comes and they don't get out of bed or the Sunday chosen for cleaning has suddenly been designated a brunch and shopping day with friends. So for many, junk rooms, closets, and drawers stay as they are, which does not stop gay hearts from dreaming of opening the door to their junk room, spraying the room with lighter fluid, tossing in a lit match, and then slamming the door. Out of sight, out of mind. At least until company arrives.

METROSEXUALS

Gay hearts are happy that their straight friends have cleaned up their acts, but they weep over the consequences this transformation has caused. At first glance, it's now nearly impossible to tell who is gay and who isn't, making for embarrassing hookup fails as gay hearts inadvertently attempt to pick up a dude they had no idea was merely a metrosexual. Gay boy hearts weep with confusion at the likes of David Beckham, Dr. Robert Rey, Ryan Seacrest, George Clooney, Pete Wentz, and Zac Efron. Please, go get some cigars and stop looking so damn pretty.

TRAINWRECK BRITNEY

Photo by petercruise

Ever since she appeared out of nowhere in a schoolgirl outfit telling everyone to hit her one more time, many gay hearts fell in love with Britney Spears—hitting her millions of times by downloading her CDs and dancing at her concerts. Heralded as the new Madonna at one time, and a supporter of gay marriage, Britney even had gay hearts aflutter when she lip-locked Madonna with a French kiss at the MTV awards. But then she crashed hard, and the Britney that gay hearts cherished so much disappeared in a sad trail of bizarre events and paparazzi following her around, doing stupid stuff while shopping and clubbing. Gay hearts weep for trainwreck Britney and pray those days are gone and she will reclaim her reign as a fabulous beloved pop diva. Gay hearts leave Britney this message: No more crazy! Come back to us so we can stop weeping.

70 DIETS THAT DON'T WORK

Gay hearts will try any diet fad to lose those unwanted pounds, but the weeping begins after they spend hundreds of dollars on peanut butter, bananas, tuna fish, lemonade, cabbage, cookies, and water pills only to then discover that they are heavier than when they started. Gay hearts yearn for the day when a real diet plan comes along that not only works but allows them to eat and drink whatever they want, watch as much TV as they want, and sleep as long as they want. Until that pill shows up, the gay heart will weep over poundage gains and wish they had the chutzpa to stick their finger down their throat.

THE WEEPIEST DIET FADS EVER

- The Master Cleanse
- The Tapeworm Diet
- Ab belts
- The General Motors (GM) Diet
- Magical walking shoes
- The Alkaline Diet
- Ayds Weight-Loss Candy
- Soaps and creams claiming
  to melt the fat off
- The Grapefruit Diet
- The Taco Bell Drive-Thru Diet
- Kimkins
- The Baby Food Diet
- The Special K Cereal Diet
- The Pregnant Lady Pee Diet

71 WEARING FLIP-FLOPS WITH SOCKS

Gay hearts weep in horror at people who wear socks with their flip-flops. They don't understand why someone would want his feet to resemble camel toes. And why is this person wearing socks in ninety-degree weather? Does he have a skin condition? Why doesn't this sock lover just choose to wear a fashionable shoe like some Chucks or Keds? Could wearing flip-flops with socks really just mean the person can't afford to buy shoes? Whatever the case, gay hearts weep over these sock-wearing flip-flopping individuals. And that weeping quickly turns to sobbing if they accidentally encounter a fat dude on a beach wearing a purple and yellow striped Speedo along with bright orange socks and black flip-flops. A sight like this only means one thing for gay hearts (and probably straight hearts, too): the end of the world is near.

72 NOT WEARING A HALLOWEEN COSTUME

Halloween is the biggest night of the year for gay hearts, so it should come as no surprise that they weep like a witch without a broomstick when they arrive at a party or street festival looking all fabulous as Dolly Parton or Captain Jack and then find themselves surrounded by a crowd of spectators doing the come-as-you-are show. While some gay hearts get pissy over throngs of people not wearing costumes on Halloween, there are other gay hearts—mostly the drag queens with big hair and big dresses—who aren't nearly so weepy about it because they love being the center of attention and they don't care who's taking the picture as long as they are striking poses and the flash bulbs are snapping.

73 STANDING IN LINE

Perhaps more than any other culture, gay hearts weep over having to stand in line. *Any* line. Long or short. Doesn't matter. Weeping will commence. Melissa Etheridge or Neil Patrick Harris could be at the end of the line handing out personal invitations to a private dinner party and gay hearts would still sigh and say, "Why is this line so long? Why do I have to wait?" They will then begin plotting how they can get to the front of the line. This entails asking everyone around who is in charge and then using some clever made-up line about why they should go ahead of everyone else (I'm handicapped, a famous drag queen, or the nephew of the owner). If that doesn't work, some douchey gay hearts will then attempt to cut. But that doesn't sit well with other gay hearts who have to wait because their plan to get ahead didn't work either, and the weeping from having to stand in line suddenly turns into a full-on temper tantrum, Mel Gibson style!

TEN PLACES WHERE GAY HEARTS WEEP ABOUT HAVING TO STAND IN LINE

1. New video game releases
2. Entrance of Gay Pride festival
3. Discount stores
4. Coffee shop
5. Box office
6. Costco
7. Drag queen meet and greet
8. Summer blockbuster movies
9. Bathroom at the mall
10. To buy the new iPhone

74 CREEPY MOTELS

Nothing freaks out gay hearts more than having to spend the night at a dirty ramshackle motel that looks like a place they could be murdered in. They've seen too many horror movies and they all know how *Psycho* ends. A gay heart will never intentionally plan on spending the night in a creepy motel. It almost always happens by accident, when fate delivers an obstacle in the form of a snowstorm, broken-down car, lack of funds, or the worst of all: a blackout from doing too many drugs and alcohol. Waking up to stains in the ceiling, orange floral curtains that match the comforter, and the smell of a dingy mildewy rug doesn't just make them weep, it makes them scream as they grab their clothes and run from the death-trap room half naked. If a gay heart in need of a room can't find a nearby Sheraton or Holiday Inn, and his only option is a creepy motel, more often than not he'll opt to spend the night in the car, with the doors locked and the keys in the ignition. He may wake up the next morning weeping with back pain, but it beats risking a re-enactment of a scene from *Deliverance*.

75 TRUE BLOOD AND DEXTER SPOILERS

Many gay hearts are huge fans of the TV shows *True Blood* and *Dexter*, so it is always best to use caution when talking to them the day after one of these shows airs. Always ask first, "Hey, did you catch *True Blood* last night?" A gay heart fang-banger fan will immediately say yes, and respond with something like "It was amazing, and that scene with Bill and Sam left me wanting to take a cold shower." But if the gay heart had to work late or go to his mother's birthday dinner and he hasn't seen the episode yet and you let loose something like "Can you believe it? Bill and Sam made out . . ." there will be gay heart weeping hell to pay! Spoilers beware! Gay hearts may do more than just weep if you ruin important plot twists on their favorite shows, especially when those shows involve vampires and serial killers.

THE CHICKEN DANCE

If asked to do the Chicken Dance at a corporate meeting, at a birthday party, or on a dare, a gay heart will weep like a chicken as they bend their arms into the shape of wings, bob their head, and stick their butts out in the air like they are about to sit on the crapper. Gay hearts love to dance and they'll shake their booty and wave their arms to a variety of dance moves (except the Macarena—a gay heart will never do the Macarena). Give them Vogue, the Electric Slide, the Robot, Line Dancing, the Time Warp, Walking Like an Egyptian, or even the new Tightrope, but not some barnyard poultry routine that even Big Bird would scoff at. Gay hearts are completely puzzled (and weepy) over those morons who shout out, "Hey everybody, let's do the Chicken Dance!" They don't understand why anyone would want to strut around like a strung-out pterodactyl with a pole shoved up its ass. The Chicken Dance was meant to be performed in only one place: kindergarten—right before nap time.

TEN WEEPIEST DANCES EVER

1. The Macarena
2. Walking like an Egyptian
3. The robot
4. The running man
5. The sprinkler
6. The wop
7. Swaying back and forth
8. The worm
9. Slam dancing (moshing)
10. Any square dance

SHOE VIOLATIONS

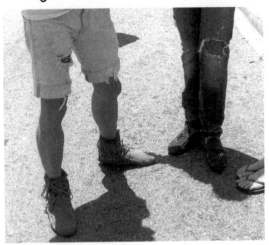

Let the weeping begin when gay hearts spot shoe violations walking down the street. While improper usage of Uggs and Crocs make them weepy no matter what the person is wearing (and it's usually atrocious), certain types of shoes should not be worn with certain kinds of outfits:

- Stilettos with "Daisy Dukes" (cut-off denim shorts)
- Doc Martens worn with anything, but especially not with dresses
- Men's dress shoes with black socks and board shorts
- Dress slacks with flip-flops (with or without socks)
- Converse Chucks with a dress
- Tracksuits with heels or dress shoes
- White go-go boots with Capri pants
- Flats with an evening gown
- Moccasin boots with shorts in 100-degree heat (pictured here)

Many gay hearts are perpetrators of wearing the wrong shoes. No one really knows for sure why. It could have to do with an overconfident sense of fashion that suddenly makes any pairing of shoe and outfit look fabulous. This always backfires the next day when the gay heart sees a photo of himself on Facebook at a party wearing orange Crocs with his übercool Rock & Republic jeans. Gay heart weeping will commence as he deletes the photo and tosses the Crocs in a box headed for Out of the Closet thrift store.

WEEPIEST SHOE TRENDS

- Chinese slippers
- Men's dressy sandals
- Jellies
- Shoes with built-in socks
- Clark's Wallabee shoes
- Platform sneakers
- High-heel sneakers
- Wheelies
- Clogs
- Dr. Scholl's wooden sandals
- Furry boots
- Boots covered in fringe
- Birkenstocks
- Whore boots (thigh-high stiletto boots)
- High-heel shoes with pockets

FOOD NETWORK ADDICTION

Hungry gay hearts in love with everything having to do with food cannot stop watching the Food Network. They devour the competitiveness of *Iron Chef*, the *Next Food Network Star*, and *Cupcake Wars*. They laugh and salivate watching the very funny and charismatic Paula Deen whip up artery-clogging macaroni and cheese in a Crock-Pot.

And although *Diners, Drive-ins, and Dives* causes gay hearts to snarl their lips with an ewwww as they gasp at scary delicacies such as fried butter in places that look like they should be condemned, the actual Food Network weeping comes with the realization that even though they spend countless hours watching spectacular and sometimes easy dishes prepared right in front of their eyes by the likes of Emeril and Rachael Ray, gay hearts will never in a million years actually make anything they've watched on the Food Network, it's just too much work. Takeout will have to do.

THE TEXTING-CHALLENGED

It's no secret that a gay heart texts more than a teenage girl hiding under the covers in her bedroom at one in the morning. This is why gay hearts weep for the texting-challenged. When one of their friends or relatives informs them "I don't text," the gay heart quickly replies, "I don't talk, so if you want to reach me, have one of your friends send me a text." It's annoying for both parties, but if you want to communicate with a gay heart you must be adept at texting.

Not being adept at texting is another issue gay hearts weep over. It's is nearly impossible to decipher any text message sent by a textard—a person who is texting with half his brain missing, failing miserably at being able to write a simple sentence and spell a simple word like "you." He hits the send button without rereading what he wrote, which almost always elicits a "wtf?" from the gay heart trying to decode the textard's message. A simple text that should read "I just picked up fluffy from the vet. Will be there in 20" ends up reading "piked veat fluf. wl b 20," Gay hearts weep for textards and hope that one day the Sylvan Learning Center will begin teaching texting classes so they can sign up all their friends and relatives.

80 NOT OWNING A TV

Gay hearts weep HD Digital tears of sympathy for anyone who lives in this world without a television. They certainly can't! Missing such gay-heart fan fare as *Glee*, *True Blood*, *Desperate Housewives*, *Spartacus*, *The Real L Word*, and *Dancing with the Stars*, or not being able to channel surf Logo, Style, Food Network, Showtime, HBO, and beloved Bravo, would be such a devastating entertainment catastrophe, their boob tube brains can't even fathom the kind of dry-heave weeping it would cause. You will never see gay hearts without some sort of access to TV shows via their iPhone, laptop, or one of the numerous televisions they have positioned throughout their home. Not owning a TV is a very dangerous position for gay hearts to be in because it could lead to TV-mooching off friends, neighbors, and people they don't like, and extended prime-time visits to Best Buy.

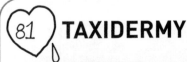

8.1 ♥ TAXIDERMY

Seeing someone's beloved dead Chihuahua, Brutus, stuffed like a beanie baby wearing a pink Juicy Couture sweater, eerily grinning with his tongue out while standing guard in the entryway of a home, will definitely freak out many gay hearts and make them weep from the pure shock of it! While a gay heart can understand why someone would want to immortalize a three-dimensional memory of a beloved little pet, should she randomly encounter a creepy room full of multiple heads from Bambi, Simba, Tigger, and Big Bird staring back at her from mounted wood plaques, there will be hell to pay. Gay hearts weep for these poor defenseless woodland creatures that now serve as interior gargoyles disturbing the shit out of whoever lays eyes on them.

LIVING IN A BAD PART OF TOWN

While gay hearts love to surround themselves with beauty and inspiration, and will create a fabulous home no matter where they live, it's no secret they would rather live in a refrigerator box in Beverly Hills than a mansion on a street that looks like a backdrop for the movie *Slumdog Millionaire*. Graffiti-stained walls, gang activity, trash-filled streets, unruly rugrats, and homeless people are enough to make any gay heart weep as they get in the habit of running from their car to their front door every day. While they weep over having to live in a shithole of an area, they find comfort in the belief that their weeping won't be for long because of what's known as gay gentrification. As more of their gay heart brothers and sisters buy homes in the so-called scary area and move in, a beautification takes place, an actual gaytrification! Graffiti walls get a glitter glam treatment making them look like art, festive gay pride block parties scare the shit out of gangs, gay hearts pay unruly rugrats to pick up trash, and re-landscaping occurs that's so perfectly stunning, it would bring a tear to Martha Stewart's eyes. Slowly but surely, the gay goes from weeping about living in a bad part of town to smiling about showcasing on Wisteria Lane.

MUFFIN TOPS

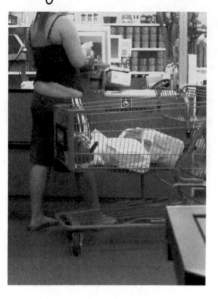

Whenever gay heart eyes are accosted by the sight of a muffin top waddling proudly down the street like Daisy Duck in a bikini, not only do they weep, they quickly search for some kind of jacket, blanket, or plastic tarp to cover up the flabby offender while Googling the nearest doctor who can perform lap band surgery. It's been reported that weeping gay hearts across many states are in the final stages of revealing Proposition 500 Pounds, which takes aim at the muffin top street epidemic, making it illegal for fat people to randomly show up at public places wearing tight-fitting pants that push revolting folds of stomach lard over their waistbands. Opponents of the proposition believe it could cause flash mobs of angry muffin tops to strike at any time and also put the website People of WalMart out of business. But gay hearts stand strong on the issue with their no-muffin campaign: Muffin tops don't seep, gay hearts won't weep.

84 OVERPRICED COFFEE DRINKS

Gay hearts weep for the $5 latte that doesn't taste any better than that cup of instant coffee grandpa was peddling in the "Instant Coffee" entry. Sure, the place added an extra shot of espresso, soy milk, and maybe some weird fanciful bacon-flavored syrup, but does that justify a pricetag of more than $5? No flipping way. Gay hearts weep for overpriced coffee drinks for a couple of reasons: First, they know they'll need another one in about an hour; and second, they don't come with alcohol (which would actually make the $5 worth it).

TOO MUCH AUTO-TUNE

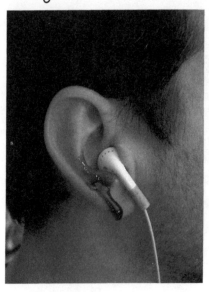

Gay hearts love them some Auto-Tune—when used sparingly, like when Cher gets a momentary electronic shot making her sound like a disco fembot while she croons "Do you belieeeeeeeeeeeeeeve!" But gay hearts' weeping turns into a synthesized wail when their ears are assaulted by too much Auto-Tune, making a normally awesome artist like Usher suddenly sound like a broken *Star Wars* droid singing through a harmonica. It's annoying and should be used only as background music for nightclub scenes in bad science fiction movies.

THE KARDASHIANS

Gay hearts are so sick of seeing the Kardashians everywhere that they not only weep, but they want to puke. This special kind of Kardashian puke is not unlike what happens after eating too much chocolate or drinking too much beer, and is the result of being bombarded (usually not by choice) with this astronomically annoying and ticky-tacky clan. Kardashian TV shows. Kardashian asses being showcased. Kardashians pushing weight-loss programs. Kardashians on talk shows. Kardashians dancing. Kardashians selling clothes. Kardashians promoting cupcakes. Kardashians having babies. Kardashians on TMZ. Kardashians getting married. Kardashians writing books about what they have learned. Kardashians hawking jewelry. Kardashians at movie premieres. Kardashians whoring out skin care. Kardashians singing with Auto-Tune. Kardashians striking poses on the beach. Kardashians chasing Justin Bieber on the beach. Kardashians at basketball, football, baseball, and soccer events. Kardashians on restroom stall doors.

On days when the Kardashian assault is intense, the gay heart puking can be more horrible than the worst stomach flu. A trip to the ER is highly recommended (as long as it's a Kardashian-free zone, which can be hard to find sometimes).

REALITY SHOWS AND STARS THAT MAKE GAY HEARTS WEEP

- *My Super Sweet Sixteen*
- *Flavor of Love* and *Flavor Flave*
- Entire cast of *Jersey Shore* (but gay hearts secretly like them)
- Heidi Montag and Spencer Pratt
- *Who Wants to Marry a Multi-millionaire*
- *The Bachelors* (all of them)
- *The Swan*
- *Jon & Kate Plus Eight*
- *Temptation Island*

MORE REALITY SHOWS AND STARS THAT MAKE GAY HEARTS WEEP

- All recent Survivors
- *Pretty Wild* (Alexis Neiers and Gabby Neiers)
- *Farmer Wants a Wife*
- *I'm a Celebrity . . . Get Me Out of Here*
- Tori and Dean
- *Celebrity Apprentice*
- *Are You Hot?*

87 PEOPLE WHO DON'T HUG

Gay hearts love to hug it out. They weep for those terrified non-huggers who stand frozen at attention with their arms at their sides like they're worried something scary will emerge from their armpits if they attempt an embrace. It is truly tragic. Gay hearts, on the other hand, are equal-opportunity huggers and will wrap their arms around just about anyone . . . unless your name is Ann Coulter.

ALTERNATIVE MOVEMENTS FOR PEOPLE WHO DON'T LIKE TO BE HUGGED

- Euro air kiss
- Limp handshake
- High-five
- Bone-crusher handshake
- Pinky swear
- Finger-grab handshake
- Beauty pageant wave
- Peace sign
- Vulcan salute
- The bird

88 GETTING CAUGHT WEARING THE SAME CLOTHES TWO DAYS IN A ROW

Gay hearts weep when an attentive friend suddenly notices they are breaking fashion's cardinal rule and committing a Lady Ga Ga sin by wearing the same clothes two days in a row. Whatever the reason for the image misstep—laundry needs to be done, no time to pick out a new outfit, or just come from a one night stand's house, the moment a gay heart is caught wearing the same clothes two days in a row is one of those light bulb moments. Many will realize that people who live in glass fashion houses should not throw Prada stones. So the next time a gay heart notices a coworker or friend who has not changed their threads in two days, he is much more understanding because he appreciates there has to be an uncontrollable circumstance involved as to why the fashion faux pas occurred. And it's up to him to find out what it was, especially if it involves something juicy like a booty call.

89 BLACKOUT DRINKING

Gay hearts love socializing and hanging out with friends at a bar and trying every wild named shot under the alcoholic rainbow. Bring on the Jell-O shots, Raspberry Lemonade Kamikazes, Brain Erasers, Scooby Snacks, Cement Mixers, Buttery Nipples, Flaming Dr. Pepper Shots, and the Rocky Mountain Bear Fuckers! The wilder the name and color, the more they want it. But like all nights of hard drinking, sometimes the next shot doesn't involve tequila; instead, it's a shot to the head in the form of a full-on blackout. And the gay heart weeping begins the next morning when they wake up dazed and confused and half naked on a stranger's couch wearing a pink page boy wig and covered in magic marker graffiti.

WATCHING MADONNA FROM THE NOSEBLEED SECTION

Madonna goes with gay like green olives go with a dirty martini. You can't have one without the other! Not only has the iconic pop legend been a huge supporter of the gay community from day one, when there weren't many celebrity supporters, but her elaborate live performances evoke the kind of concert-going spectacle no gay heart would miss in a trillion years.

So when magical Madge (or Esther, as she is known by some) comes to town, the gay-heart stampede to get the best tickets is nothing short of a *who-has-the-most-money-and-the-best-ticket-broker* cage fight. To afford Madonna tickets, gay hearts will go to extreme measures like maxing out their credit cards, forgoing tanning, manicures, and chemical peels, giving up coffee shop lattes for a year, canceling HBO and Showtime indefinitely, and attempting to return as many overpriced designer clothes as they can. If the gay heart can't swing the $800 tickets to sit at the edge of the catwalk and get sprayed with Madonna sweat, they will take whatever available spot they can, just so long as they are in the same room dancing. This airy-fairy, happy-just-to-be-in-Madonna's-presence attitude will last only until moments before the show when the gay heart finds $250 tickets are so far up the nosebleed section they can actually touch the ceiling of the auditorium with the palm of their hand.

Uncontrollable and often over melodramatic weeping will follow as the gay heart prepares to compare the Polly Pocket-looking Madonna doll on stage to the big screen TV version over the stage. Although the gay heart is relieved they will see their beloved Madonna's face, they are quite concerned about the nosebleed ceiling inches from their head and how they will keep from injuring themselves when the gay high priestess starts to sing "Vogue."

91 UGLY TRAMP STAMPS

When it comes to tattoos, nothing will make a gay heart weep faster than catching sight of an ugly tramp stamp—a notoriously slutty tat drawn right above the butt crack. If someone is wearing a crop top or short tee and they bend over, the tramp stamp will be visible for the entire world to see (and weep over, if that's the case). Even though some tramp stamps can be sexy, 99.9 percent of them are skanky and revolting, and usually the kind of person sporting one also has rolls of fat to support the tat above their crack.

THE WEEPIEST TRAMP STAMP TRENDS

- **Thongs:** It's bad enough a real thong can be seen from a muffin top and low-rise jeans, but there are those who have taken to tattooing one in the same vicinity—just in case(?).
- **Presidents:** Obama Girl, Bush Country, Ronald Reagan 1911–2004—*so* not sexy.
- **Horror Movies:** Jason's hockey mask, Freddy Kreuger's pitted face, chainsaw spouting blood—*also* not sexy.
- **Alien Sex Fantasies:** Two-headed chick monster licking a giant penis—scary.
- **Mentioning the Parents:** I ←3 Mom and Dad—stupid.
- **Religious Verses:** The Bible or the Koran—a verse from either should *not* appear on someone's ass.
- **Sex Phrases:** "Insert coins into slot" or "Free mustache rides"—pathetic.

Gay hearts not only weep over hideous tramp stamps but for those amazing ink artists who have to clean up someone else's terrible tattoo. Somewhere Kat Von D is reaching for a bottle of vodka.

When gay hearts see hoarders on Oprah or the *Hoarders* TV show and they take in the shocking footage of homes turned into land- fills, they weep for those over- whelmed squirrel people saving shit they don't need. They weep also because they know they have parents or relatives who do the exact same thing and they fear that one day, if they are not careful, their gay hearts will end up on a show called *Gay Hoarders* with someone like Ty Pennington forcing them to haul all of their shit onto the front lawn and put it in piles for charity and garage sales. For a hoarding gay heart who weeps uncontrol- lably about getting rid of anything, the stasher piles would look something like this:

- Mounds of Madonna and Cher memorabilia
- Enough Disneyland memorabilia to open a store *inside* of Disneyland
- Overflowing tubs of Melissa Etheridge Memorabilia (gay heart girls)
- Stacks of boxes containing drag queen accessories—wigs, makeup, clothes (gay heart boys)
- Motorcycles and accessories (gay heart girls)
- Shopping bags full of VHS and DVD porn videos (gay heart boys)
- Shopping bags full of Lesbian romance novels (gay heart girls)

- A mountainous pile the size of Mt. Everest composed of "never before worn" or "worn only once" clothes, accessories, and shoes from various discount stores and designer boutiques
- Hundreds of Target bags holding never-used random things like napkin rings, shower curtain liners, office supplies, and waste baskets
- Collectible dolls from favorite TV shows and movies like *Star Trek*, *Zena*, *Nightmare Before Christmas*, and *Star Wars*
- Piles of dog and cat accessories, including clothes, food dishes, chew toys, and catnip toys
- Shopping bags full of Gay Pride freebies (packets of rubbers and lube, gay yellow pages, and ugly free T-shirts from some rave event)
- Heaps of crap from Home Depot or Lowe's (stuff like random lumber, weird tools, gardening supplies, and creepy gnomes)
- Loads of IKEA furniture bought without having a place for it
- Hundreds of useless antique items that were purchased on weekend antiquing trips
- Enough Halloween and Christmas decorations to adorn the Playboy Mansion and all the homes surrounding it

RAINBOW-COLORED FOOD

While being lovers of pretty much anything rainbow, gay hearts do, however, weep with foodie fright when they are presented with rainbow-colored eats: rainbow cakes and cupcakes with rainbow frosting and sprinkles, rainbow tie-dye-looking bagels, pancake short stacks in the colors of the rainbow, cinnamon rolls in rainbow twists, rainbow macaroni, rainbow candy, or one of the newest rainbow-colored food inventions: bacon strips. Gay hearts aren't weeping so much for the colorful presentation and playfulness of rainbow food; the weeping has to do with the knowledge behind what makes the food transform into such vibrant rainbow colors. It's the realization that any kind of food looking so rainbow-tastic could not *possibly* be good for you. Not all gay hearts weep over rainbow food though. When presented with a syrup-covered short stack of rainbow pancakes, one gay heart will see beautiful gay yummy rainbow colors, while the other will see scary chemical-bows of Red Dye #40, Yellow Dye #4, and Blue Dye #1.

94 CUDDLE PARTIES

If a gay heart is invited to a cuddle party, he will think it's some kind of pajama rave and say "Sure! Sounds fun let's hit Macy's for new pajamas and then the liquor store!" But when he finds out that a cuddle party is not a drunken theme bash, but actually a therapy-type session where men and women face their intimacy issues by gathering in a group, wearing pajamas or sweats, and spooning each other for several hours, he'll weep in complete and utter shock. And wonder if cuddle parties are a breeding ground for space invaders. Why would someone want to inhale someone else's b.o. and feel their body fat? Weeping gay hearts go ewwwwww. Not to mention that cuddle parties look like giant orgies except everyone is clothed and there is no sex. Not even dry humping. Yes, once the gay heart finds out what a cuddle party really is he will suddenly have a weepy excuse as to why he won't be able to attend. No alcohol and having to stay completely clothed the whole time? Forget it.

KISSY-FACE PHOTOS

Gay hearts weep with puckering horror whenever they see a photo of one or more people extending their lips into a giant puffy purse looking like they overdosed on collagen injections. Weeping gay hearts feel that kissy-face poseurs and their deformed looking lips should be held accountable for the reactions their photos cause and they should be required by law to pay for kissy-face therapy sessions to anyone who has been victimized by their obscene lips, including traumatized little children, old people, and observant dogs.

96 CREDIT CARD DENIED

Like everyone else, gay hearts are embarrassed when their credit card is denied. But when it's denied after standing in line for hours waiting for Lady Gaga tickets and they are lucky enough to win the Ticketmaster lotto and the computer pulls up front row center seats, and they have no other credit card or source of instant funds to save the gaytastic seats they just scored, the tantrum weeping will begin. And it won't be pretty, sounding like Gaga herself at the beginning of *Bad Romance*, only as if it were being sung by a werewolf: "Rawr-rawr-ah-ah-ah! roma-roma-mamaaaaaa! Ga-ga-ooh-la-la! I WANT LADY GAGA TICKETS!"

97 NOT BEING ABLE TO FIT IN YOUR FAVORITE DESIGNER JEANS

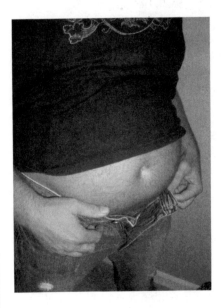

When the fateful day comes that a gay heart is no longer able to fit into his favorite designer jeans he will weep while sucking his gut in. As he peels the useless $250 jeans from his body he will vow to get to the gym he never uses. This will be followed up by Googling the latest diet fad they hope involves a pill and chocolate. Sadly the favorite jeans will be folded up and put back in the closet with the promise to wear them again when the weight is down. (This kind of wishful thinking can often be the first step toward becoming a gay hoarder.) While gay hearts weep over not being able to fit into jeans that caused them to eat celery for a month, they always try to see the bright rainbow side of things. And in this case, it means they get to go shopping!

98 CELEBRITY PERFUMES

Gay hearts weep every time there is an announcement about another lame celebrity coming out with another stinky fragrance. The perfume industry is so eager to use a hot name on their bottle of make-you-vomit-sugary-fermented-orange-musk scent, they will hand it off to anyone who has a CD or cable show and let them create a stupid-ass title. Does the world really need another grossly sweet perfume by the Kardashians, Paris Hilton, Miley Cyrus, or Britney Spears? And is the world ready for gagging scents from Kristen Stewart, Shawn Johnson, and Justin Bieber? Nauseated weeping gay hearts say NO! They would rather spray themselves with eau de rhinoceros ball sweat.

WEEPIEST THINGS TO BUY AT THE MALL

- Pretzels because they make you fat, but you have to have one anyway
- Expensive beauty products that the specialist said would make you look ten years younger, all at the bargain cost of a thousand dollars
- Cheap underwear on sale you will never wear
- Flavored condoms that will be thrown away after they've expired
- More than one As Seen on TV product
- A $5 coffee drink loaded with sugar and caffeine because you need to keep going, need to keep shopping
- Overpriced jeans that will be out of style and marked down in a month
- A hot dog on a stick
- Another trendy $50 T-shirt you'll wear once and forget you have
- A fugly pair of kelly green Chucks because they were on sale
- Gift cards for someone else

99 GETTING TO A SALE TOO LATE

Everybody loves a good sale, except for a weeping gay heart who slept in and showed up at the Nordstrom Anniversary Sale three hours too late and missed all of the good bargains. Weepy sales are the worst for gay hearts because so many of them consider themselves to be hard-core shoppers who get the best fashions and find the best deals. Sale shopping can also cause a lot of whining because they feel that since they are in a store at a big sale they can't leave until they make a purchase. This leads to even more weeping and whining when they become frustrated about not finding anything awesome on sale in their size and they turn to the regular-priced racks where there are a plethora of choices waiting to be snatched up. Three shopping bags later and none of it on sale, they are headed out the door as happy gay hearts, eager to put on a hot new outfit and go out. For gay hearts it's all about living in the moment: they will hold back the weeping for what they've done until the credit card bill arrives.

(100) BIKRAM YOGA

A gay heart will try anything once, especially if it's related to health and looking hot. So it's no surprise that if invited to attend a Bikram Yoga class, unaware gay hearts will say, "Sure I've always wanted to try yoga. I hear it's great." However, when they find out that Bikram Yoga takes place in a room with no open windows or doors in 105 degree heat, the weeping will commence, followed by the questions "Do they have it available with air-conditioning?" and "Can I bring a Big Gulp?"

(101) FOX NEWS

Although gay hearts don't watch Fox News, they definitely weep for its homophobic rhetoric. Their cast of colorful offending journalists (you know this bunch: Bill O'Reilly, Mike Huckabee, Sean Hannity, and Glenn Beck) spout hateful, rude remarks about gay people any time they want. And lots of times when the nasty comments from these ignoramuses are picked up by the media, they quickly tell everyone to lighten up, they were only making a joke! This heinous homophobic behavior makes gay hearts especially weepy because some of their favorite shows air on Fox, like *American Idol*, *The Simpsons*, *Family Guy*, and *Glee*, and they can't help but wonder if Fox corporate is saying we love and support the gays when they're singing, dancing, and making everyone laugh for ratings, but not when it comes to the serious stuff. So with Fox News proudly proclaiming they are a "fair and balanced" news network, owner Rupert Murdoch should change the slogan to The "Shits and Giggles" Fox News Network. That way, when Bill O'Reilly wants to compare a gay person to a terrorist and call it a joke, gay hearts won't care because they know the network's a joke.

102 PANT VIOLATIONS

Gay hearts believe that if you're gonna hang out in your own home, feel free to wear your comfy stars-and-stripes MC Hammer pants all you want. Do a little hammer-time if you want. No one will see you but your pets (although they might run under the bed). But stepping out in public looking like a 4th of July Aladdin parade balloon will not only cause a gay heart to weep but force him to call the National Fashion Guard to have you and your pants removed from public display.

Gay hearts weeping over hideous pant violations would like to offer this tip if you are unsure about your pant choice: If the first thing that comes to your mind when you see yourself in the mirror is related to Halloween, sci-fi, or WTF?, take your pants off immediately and burn them. Remember, the pant police are watching.

WEEPY PANT VIOLATIONS

- Leggings as pants

- Sausage-like bodies stuffed into skinny jeans

- Stirrup pants

- Low low-rise jeans

- Harem pants (also known as MC Hammer or parachute pants)

- Mom and dad jeans (high-waist jeans with tapered leg)

- Pajama bottoms worn outside the house

- All Capri pants in any fabric or length

- Shorts or Capri pants worn with jackets

- Wide-legged oversized jeans

- Skin tight peg-legged pants

- Baggy jeans worn backward

- Overalls worn anywhere outside the barnyard

(103) REAL HOUSEWIVES WITHDRAWAL

Gay hearts love to watch a good suburban cat fight! That's why they can't get enough of Bravo's Housewives. New Jersey, Orange County, Atlanta, D.C., Beverly Hills, or New York—doesn't matter, gay hearts love them all. Beside being fashion divas, Bravo's illustrious housewives always provide surprises, whether it's Teresa calling Danielle a prostitution whore and flipping a table at a restaurant, Kelly going mental on an island and calling Bethenny a hobag, Nene going ballistic on the street calling Kim a whole bunch of names and trying to pull her wig off, Danielle getting her weave yanked out at a fashion show by Jacqueline's daughter, or just crazy Ramona being crazy by strutting down the catwalk at a fashion show looking like she's possessed by a robot. The housewives never fail to entertain a gay heart, so it should come as no surprise within minutes of the season finale reunion show's ending, gay hearts are weeping and shaking with Housewives Withdrawal. They watched so much backstabbing, bitching, name-calling, and hair-pulling, that suddenly having nothing juicy like that to watch and talk about with friends can plunge a gay heart deep into cable television depression. Thankfully Bravo has started scheduling their Housewives shows to overlap so when one is ending another is starting. This makes gay hearts everywhere housewife happy and keeps any sudden weeping directed at bad fashion or singing.

104) TOO MUCH PLASTIC AND BOTOX

Although many gay hearts approve of selective plastic surgery and Botox because they want to continue looking fabulous as they age, they weep for those unhappy women (and some men) out there who have such low self-esteem about their already beautiful bodies, and have become so addicted to the knife and go to such extremes with the needle, they end up looking like a shiny bloated Muppet with alien eyes and permanent kissy-face lips. Gay hearts weep for plastic Botox Muppet Heidi Montag, who has had up to ten surgeries in one day. She claims she does it to become the "best me," but gay hearts want Heidi to know her "best me" is found by sculpting one's self on the inside, not on a surgical table in Beverly Hills. But nevertheless, should Heidi wake up one day twenty years from now and find her body taking on that unnatural puffy poultry look from too much plastic and Botox like scary plastic surgery nightmare Jocelyn Wildenstein, gay hearts also want Heidi to know she always has the option to change her body's appearance, and she would be welcomed with open arms into the transgender community. She'd make quite a beautiful man.

105 TACKY HOME DÉCOR

Gay hearts weep with wide eyes when they encounter really shitty home décor. They feel there's absolutely no excuse for walking into a living room that looks like a '70s thrift store/drug dealer's den. Overly sensitive gay hearts can also be disturbed at the sight of figurines everywhere, plastic fruit, wood paneling, snow globe collections, and family picture frame overload. Gay hearts feel in today's world it's just not acceptable to invite people over to homes that look like that. There is plenty of interior decorating help out there from HGTV, *Extreme Makeover: Home Edition*, IKEA, Target, Michaels, Home Depot, Lowe's, and a billion other stores and thrift shops. Not to mention the slew of friends and neighbors that would love to help so they can actually come to visit more often. Should someone with shitty home décor have difficulty changing it on their own, gay hearts recommend they contact designer Nate Berkus immediately. He'll be happy to bulldoze their storage shed of a mancave.

TOP TEN DÉCOR OFFENSES

1. Popcorn ceilings
2. Orange shag carpet
3. Plastic on furniture
4. Many animal prints and figurines
5. Pee-stained carpeting
6. La-Z-Boy recliners
7. Wood paneling
8. Knickknack overload
9. Plastic patio chairs, beach chairs, and folding chairs and tables for furniture
10. High school and college memorabilia

106 UGLY TROPHY JACKETS

Gay hearts weep when they are blinded by an ugly trophy jacket that often is made by a famous designer (cough—Dolce & Gabbana —cough) and costs a million dollars. Many of these statement jackets have overdone beading and embroidery with such loud scary patterns the man or woman wearing one could easily scare little children or give an old person a heart attack. Gay hearts weeping over this gaudy lounge lizard look suggest that anyone owning such an explosively awful trophy jacket should do one of three things: immediately burn it, run away and join Barnum & Bailey circus, or become an air traffic controller. Blinding people out in public is just not nice.

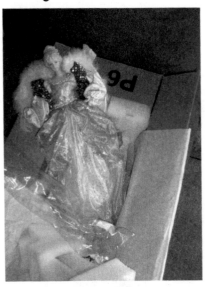

Gay hearts weep for people who spend hours in front of their TVs shopping from HSN, QVC, and lame infomercials. They weep because people who shop from TV think it's easier and they are getting better deals, but in actuality they could be screwing themselves price-wise and ordering stuff that will look like shit when they finally get it. Then there's the hassle of sending back the Slender Shaper because it didn't slenderize or the Gazelle Freestyle machine because it threw their back out. Gay hearts say it's more fun to hit the stores and get what you want, not what some cranked-up TV personality is yammering on about for half an hour. The only time shopping from TV is acceptable according to gay hearts is after the mall has closed, the Internet has gone down, and you are drinking whiskey straight out of the bottle. Shopping from TV almost can be funny and entertaining. But should one find himself in the position of wanting to buy something on TV, a tip that can curb impulse buying is to make sure all credit cards cannot be reached from the couch. This will slow things down and give you at least a few seconds to consider whether or not it's really worth stumbling off the couch to fetch your wallet. Sure, you want to buy Fluffy a new chew toy, but does it have to be that Marie Osmond doll?

108 CLOSETED CARTOON CHARACTERS

Gay hearts weep for iconic cartoon characters that must keep their gayness a secret and remain in the cartoon closet because of kiddy adoration. The following is a list of well-known characters rumored to be gay:

- Bert and Ernie
- SpongeBob SquarePants
- Patrick Starfish
- Peppermint Patty
- Charlie Brown
- Babar the Elephant
- Purple Tinky Winky
- The Smurfs (all of them)
- Waylon Smithers and Mr. Burns
- Popeye
- Snagglepuss
- Pepe Le Pew
- Hermey the Misfit Elf
- Garfield
- Scooby-Doo
- Dora the Explorer

The Simpsons™ & © Twentieth Century Fox Film Corp. All Rights Reserved.

Weeping gay hearts would like to plead with these beloved closeted toon characters (who must be very lonely and afraid) to accept their gayness and come on out of the cartoon closet! Don't worry about your careers, Logo will be happy to create shows for any of you. You'd lead happier animated lives, free to be yourselves and do whatever you wish. You could take inspiration from one of the first cartoon characters to out himself on network television: Mr. Herbert Garrison in a town called South Park. Garrison fought being gay for several seasons, constantly playing the Richard Simmons "I'm not gay" card," but then he had a nervous breakdown and ended up crazy in a cave at the top of a mountain. Thankfully Mrs. Chokesondick needed his teaching advice so Mr. Garrison became her Yoda-like teacher and ended up having a gay self-realization while inside the Tree of Insight. Besides being a place that gay hearts love, South Park is also home to Big Gay Al and Mr. Slave and they totally welcome all closeted gay cartoon characters. Except for, maybe, Stewie.

BRATTY UNATTENDED KIDS

If not parents themselves, many gay hearts are instant aunts and uncles to their friends' and relatives' kids. They love playing with their nieces and nephews, taking them shopping and to the movies, and basically spoiling them with gifts and love. But gay hearts weep with fright when they encounter unattended children running around like little possessed monsters from a low-budget horror movie. Because gay hearts are so friendly and fun, many of them become magnetic targets for these nasty little beasts and will be attacked in numerous horrific ways, such as little girls slapping them and telling them to fuck off or little boys throwing food and threatening to tie them up. Some gay hearts don't respond well to out of control rugrats strung out on kiddie coke, and they will have no problem turning into the Wicked Witch of the West threatening to summon flying monkeys that will snatch the brats up and haul them off to a dark scary cavern where they will be eaten by a two-headed dragon. Then of course the gay heart's dramatic storytelling threat suddenly freaks out the little girl with the foul mouth and she goes crying to mommy who suddenly shows up out of nowhere and proceeds to turn into super bitch and blame the gay heart for scaring her precious baby (who she wasn't even watching).

Sometimes a gay heart will get into it with the horrible parent and tell her to keep an eye on her rotten kids, but as words and accusations fly, they eventually back down when mommy rants: "What would you know about raising kids?" And if he's a single gay heart without a child or pet, he'll consider the comment. And she's right! He doesn't know shit about child raising. For most gay hearts, a run-in with a pack of badly behaved rugrats is not something they are prepared for. Having never taken any classes on child development or watched a single episode of *Super Nanny*, the only thing a gay heart should do when he encounters evil children is run for his gay life.

110 BAD KARAOKE

Whether it be at a bar, at a birthday party, or when hangin' with friends at the home pad, bad karaoke will definitely make gay hearts weep and their ears may even bleed a little, depending on how much they've had to drink. While it's true that karaoke is a fun outlet for the average Joe who likes to cut loose by pretending to be Madonna or Josh Groban, it's not always so fun for those sitting in the audience if they are being tortured by a voice that sounds like a garbage disposal with a fork stuck in it. Still, bad karaoke continues to be popular because of one reason: it's fucking hilarious. There's nothing funnier than watching a crowd egg-on a wasted person singing Mariah Carey's "Hero" while attempting to channel the diva herself and hit a high note that will probably make him choke on his spit. Watching bad karaoke is just as juicy as watching the *American Idol* rejects, only it's live and often involves best friends or a significant other, which makes a gay heart weep tears of pee-inducing laughter. In the Philippines a man was shot dead for being out of tune at a karaoke bar. Thankfully, in America it's not taken so seriously. However, bad karaoke singers should be cautious. With practically everyone having access to a video camera on their phone, YouTube is only a download away and their hideous rooster-like version of Journey's "Don't Stop Believing" will live on in infamy forever.

TOP TEN WEEPIEST KARAOKE SONGS EVER

1. Achy Breaky Heart (Billy Ray Cyrus)
2. Baby (Justin Bieber)
3. Anything by Metallica
4. Stars Are Blind (Paris Hilton)
5. America (Neil Diamond)
6. Anything by Bob Dylan
7. 867-5309/Jenny (Tommy Tutone)
8. Born in the USA (Bruce Springsteen)
9. Ice Ice Baby (Vanilla Ice)
10. Wind Beneath My Wings (Bette Midler)

(111) POTLUCKS

Whenever most gay hearts hear the word "potluck," not only do they weep, but their tummy does a little growl and says, "Don't you dare put me through that!" While a gay heart loves to plan a dinner with friends and have everyone bring a dish, especially for Oscar night, this usually involves people they know are great cooks or will bring some amazing overpriced dish from Whole Foods. The random work-related potluck is another weepy story. A coworkers' array of funky-looking dishes like casseroles resembling ground-up roadkill, neon-colored Jell-O salads, and meat and cheese platters that have turned shiny and sweaty is not a gay heart's idea of a satisfying and delicious meal. It's a breeding ground for food poisoning. And it never fails at potluck: there is always someone who does something unsanitary like toss their steak salad with their hands after wiping their nose and then offer a big mound for your plate. A gay heart's advice to surviving a potluck where you don't know the cooks all that well: stick to store-bought items like bread and corn chips. Otherwise make sure you have plenty of Immodium A-D on hand for when the diarrhea hits from the taco lasagna you begrudgingly noshed because you didn't want to piss off your boss. You'll need all the help you can get.

VISIBLE THONGS

Gay hearts weep in lingerie horror every time they see a pear-shaped woman (or man in some cases) out in public, say at a grocery store, bending over reaching for something, say a bottle of bleach, and all of a sudden she's exposing flesh, giving everyone a free showing of her nasty hot pink thong stretching out from the depths of her exposed ass crack. Other visible thong offenders are teenage girls who think butt-cleave is cool and it's hip to let their thongs hang out of their lower-than-low-cut jeans. Visible thongs are bad enough, but throw in a tramp stamp and gay hearts won't just weep, they'll want to a call 911 and have the thong-flasher arrested for offending all those innocent eyeballs that may never see clearly again.

DISCOUNT STORE SHOPPING

It's no secret most gay hearts LOVE to shop and they love a good bargain, but when it comes to discount-store shopping, it's weepy whining all the way. You see, while gay hearts are hungry for that sale price, they are not so thrilled about what they have to do to get it. Here are ten reasons gay hearts weep over discount store shopping:

1. Everything is a mess and shopping begins to feel more like digging a ditch.
2. The perfect shirt is found after hours of searching, but it's the only one and it's the wrong size.
3. Dream jeans are found at a dream price, but the dream ends in a nightmare when it's discovered the dream jeans have an irreparable hole in the crotch.
4. Shoppers throw clothes on the floor and over racks, making it difficult to shop.
5. There are no less than fifty kids running around like rabid monkeys and a baby wails at the top of its lungs every ten minutes.
6. A box of six beautiful green wine goblets that match your dinnerware are missing two and nobody knows where they are.

7. Even though the store is well-staffed and all registers are open, there are a million people in line buying and returning a million things, and the wait feels like a million years.
8. The perfect running shoes are found, only the box is holding two different sizes, and nobody knows where the other correct size is.
9. The fitting rooms look like cesspools of germs.
10. After digging through the store for five hours and trying everything on from sunglasses to shoes, the only thing purchased is a bag of off-brand chocolate-covered popcorn.

Yes, exhausted gay hearts weep over discount store shopping as they drive to designer malls and prepare to max out their cards.

(114) MOOCHERS

Most gay hearts have big hearts! And they will give the designer shirt off their back to help a friend or family member in need. The problem with owning a big gay heart that gives freely is that it can also attract big hungry moochers. Over time this can cause a gay heart to weep while being bled dry. Moochers—also known as freeloaders and leeches—will latch themselves onto a giving gay heart and take all that they can. While lying about working and usually going with a story about how they are actually rich and waiting for a fat trust fund check, moochers will ask to spend the night with the gay heart. When that happens the gay heart has been mooched! The moocher ends up attempting to stay permanently in the gay heart's house, eating all of his food, drinking all of his beer, stinking up his bathroom, watching his cable and porn, using him as a personal taxi cab, using up minutes on his phone, and asking him to pay for dinners, movies, and drinks

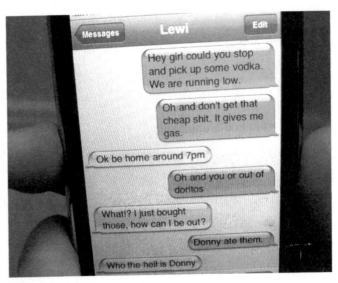

while promising to pay it all back when the big payday arrives. Moochers will also weasel their way into the gay heart's network of friends, attempt to finagle a job where the gay heart works, and in some cases hit on the gay heart's lover! After a long road of giving without question and taking it in the wallet, the moment eventually comes when the gay heart's heart—which is even bigger than Kim Kardashian's ass—explodes. Weeped out and bled dry, he ejects the moocher from his life like a festering blackhead. The way many gay hearts get rid of a moocher is usually fast and quite simple: They tell them a relative died, give the mooch a few bucks, drop him off at ritzy nightclub (where the moocher can go to work and search for a new person to suck dry) and then run off to hide in Hawaii for a week. After all they've done for that bloodsucking moocher, they deserve some leech-free R & R.

(115) EMO HAIR

Gay hearts weep blackened fearful tears for those with emo hair because not only does it remind them of David Bowie's awful hair in *Labyrinth* but they worry that emo hair can actually be a health danger! Putting aside the toxicity of the 150 kinds of color dye used for one head of hair, the real problem with emo hair has to do with the lopsided bangs. The little emo kids are destroying their eyesight by growing long strands of hair to hang over one eye while using the other to see where they are going. With such restricted eyesight, the emo is putting major strain on the only eye that can see.

This becomes particularly hazardous if they happen to be behind the wheel of their black Volkswagen beetle on the way to a My Chemical Romance concert. The possibility of hitting a parked car, old lady crossing the street, or police cruiser becomes all too great. Gay hearts weep with concern over their one-eyed emo brothers and sisters, many of whom are gay, or will be gay in the future, and feel that driving under the influence of emo bangs is a tragedy waiting to happen that could change their lives forever.

Gay hearts would like to see a personalized driving test created just for one-eyed emos with long bangs. If the emo passes the test she would be allowed to drive only Segways and Razor motor scooters. If the emo is caught breaking the law by driving under the influence of their bangs, she must face strong punishment and have her emo hair shaved completely off. It's tough love, but gay hearts feel someone has to save the emos from themselves. In a few years when they've cut their bangs off for good, they'll be grateful.

116 CREEPY OLD MEN

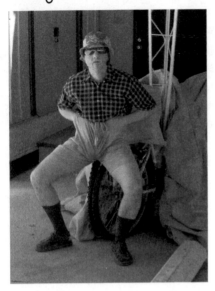

Both gay heart boys and girls weep with the willies when they encounter a creepy old man. Many gay hearts love and idolize their grandparents, so old people are especially cute to them and gay hearts will go out of their way to offer friendship and help with living needs, or just spend time visiting. Luckily there don't seem to be many creepy old ladies (or perhaps they are just better known as "hags"), but the old farts that make constant sexual jokes and can't stop staring at crotches, asses, or chests require gay hearts to keep their guard up at all times.

Although most of these creepy old men are harmless, sometimes they are not so easy to get rid of, especially if they live right next door. Since Creepy Old Man Repellent doesn't exist, gay hearts have developed several ways to rid themselves of these nasty old geezers. If you are going to a place where you may encounter a well-known creepy old man, you should bring a small bottle of body spray in a very strong floral scent or a really nasty celebrity perfume like Britney Spears's Midnight Fantasy. When creepy approaches, begin spraying the air all around. Old men can't stand strong fragrant smells and he'll shuffle away as if he's been doused in Raid bug killer. Another tactic that requires only acting is to start coughing and pretending you have the worst flu ever. Creepy old men don't want to get sick and will freak out instantly. This is an excellent way to keep them from grabbing your ass. If there isn't time for any of those protective tips to be initiated when a gay heart unexpectedly comes upon a creepy old toothless stranger sitting in his underwear and winking in a department store fitting room with the door open, the best plan of action for a weeping gay heart is one that involves running away, as fast as their gay heart can.

DISNEY LINE-CUTTERS

Line-cutters will be banished to Davey Jones Locker.

The Magic Kingdom truly is magical for gay hearts—they cherish their days with Mickey and friends at Disney World or Land. What makes them weep about the happiest place on earth is being stuck in a long line because they weren't able to get a fast pass and having some douchebag attempt to line-cut. Gay hearts don't take kindly to line-cutters, and after waiting for an hour in the blistering summer so they can take a jeep ride into Indiana's Temple of Doom (that they've taken a million times before) there are many tactics gay hearts might initiate to protect their place in line.

The first would be to cause a scene. For some gay hearts this is the easiest and most natural way to oust a line-cutter, by loudly and clearly announcing to everyone within twenty feet behind them: "I can't believe you just cut in front of all these people!" If biker dudes are standing behind them, the cutter is toast and will fly like Dumbo, but if there is a timid foreign family or a couple of teens who don't care, the gay hearts will have to resort to other maneuvers. One is to wait till they get to the front of the line and *then* expose the line-cutter, forcing them to get sent to the back of the line to start all over again.

While gay hearts usually weep over line-cutters, there is an exception to the rule when it comes to confronting Disney line-cutters. If Disney is having its popular Gay Days event and the park is jammed with gay people wearing red shirts to show gay solidarity, and a gay heart confronts a line-cutter who just happens to be a hottie wearing a red shirt, more likely than not they will let them stay, because the best thing about waiting in line at Disney during Gay Days is the cruising. It's an excellent way to get dates. Nothing weepy about that!

(118) VIRTUAL PETS

Gay hearts love their cats and dogs, so it comes as a weepy big shock when they find out their new friend's dog Ringo, a healthy two-year-old German Shepard, is not a real dog at all, but a virtual pet. What started as dress-up games for little girls has now blossomed into a full-on adult sim-like addiction: the care of fake online animals. For those longing to be pet owners but aren't, virtual pets can be adopted in a variety of species—dogs, cats, horses, turtles, monkeys, snakes, and even fish. These VPs are just as spoiled as real pets and can have their own blog and profile name, get jobs, join other pet groups, dress up in fancy clothes, and even chat with other online pets.

Gay hearts are dumbfounded over why anyone would think the image of cat on a computer screen could actually make up for the kisses and purring of a real one. But VP owners, perhaps feeling less than adequate with their handicapped pet, will attempt to convince gay hearts that they should also adopt a virtual pet, saying shit like "You really should get one, they're all the rage! You don't have to walk them or feed them. They are loyal and well-behaved at all times. You can pick out any color you want. If you dedicate enough time to its care and well-being, it will love you forever. The way you treat your pet will greatly determine how it develops and what kind of pet it will be. Show it love and it will be a great friend for you!" After barfing at statements like that, gay hearts will back away realizing perhaps they don't want to be friends with this Virtual Pet–lover any longer. While it's true Virtual Pet's have certain advantages in the virtual world that involve never getting sick or dying, or needing to have their poop picked up, they can't compare to the real-life snuggly warmth of a loving pet. Virtual Pets are weepy games for little girls.

(119) UGLY CHRISTMAS SWEATER PARTIES

When the holidays arrive most gay hearts will be invited to no fewer than five Ugly Christmas Sweater parties, and this makes them weep with a Grinchy scowl because not only are they sick of Ugly Christmas Sweater parties, but it means they will have to go out and buy no less than five new Ugly Christmas Sweaters to wear to these parties (God forbid they wear the same Ugly Christmas Sweater to more than one party).

Shopping for an Ugly Christmas Sweater can not only be daunting because all Christmas sweaters are ugly and it's difficult to decipher which is the ugliest, but it can also be hugely embarrassing—especially when the cashier says, "Aww, how cute! You will look adorable in this!" Oh sure, they had great laughs at all the previous Ugly Christmas Sweater parties, but when does the Ugly Christmas Sweater madness end, with its bad fashion and bad food? (Ugly Christmas Sweater party-throwers tend to take it over the top and serve ugly white-trash holiday food that matches the ugly sweaters.)

Must it go on year after year, forcing them to spend fifty bucks on a nasty revolting garment that they will only wear once and then throw away or send off to Goodwill? And what about all the photo-snapping that goes on at these Ugly Christmas Sweater parties? How many times will they have to keep deleting threads to friends' Facebook photo albums showing them looking more trashed than an elf the day after Christmas in a scary vest with Frosty the Snowman and Rudolph the Red-Nosed Reindeer dancing across it waving candy canes while their eyes light up in green and red? It's not a look that will get them a New Year's Eve date, and for this a gay heart weeps.

120 GUIDOS AND GUIDETTES

While many gay hearts find *Jersey Shore*'s tiny big-haired big-boobed Snooki adorable and Mike The Situation's rock-hard six-pack perfect for eating off of, when it comes to guidos and guidettes, gay hearts pretty much all agree: it's time to weep for New Jersey! And weep hard. Known to frequent Tri-State area malls, guido/guidette culture has exploded onto the pop culture scene and gay hearts are weeping more heavily than an Italian grandmother who has burned her spaghetti sauce. Guidettes are strutting around doing kissy face with their big bleached-blonde with black roots blow-out, eye makeup that would make a drag queen envious, huge fake boobs popping out of an "Italian Princess" shirt that was purchased too small, and an unnatural tan from the orange glow caused by a lethal cocktail of tanning beds and home bronzer.

A typical look for a guidette is overdosing on famous fashion designers by mixing them all together in an unsightly, pretentious manner, and they definitely like to show off bling such as a dangly silver belly button ring or a giant Playboy bunny necklace. Guidos are not far behind their girls, as they too like to sport a glowing Oompa-Loompa face, go through hundreds of jars of hair gel a week, wear tight zipper shirts, tracksuits, designer jeans, fuzzy Kangol hats, tiny hoop earrings, and fake gold chains, and they can be found slumming at their local gym tanning or lifting weights. But overall guidos don't really care about their appearance—a gut, skinny arms, tight tracksuit and sandals, so what? They still think they're the shit. The modern day guido has usually never worked a day in his life (considered among guidos as an ongoing accomplishment), which leaves him spoiled by mommy and daddy, and we can't forget how he loves to do his macho manly fist bumps. Yes, there is plenty for gay hearts to weep over whenever they catch sight of a guido or guidette. While being fascinated by Snooki and her brood, gay hearts really aren't interested in getting too close to a guido or guidette because they might suddenly be overcome with the desire to give a complete fashion makeover. What gay hearts are interested in, however, is dressing like them for Halloween.

121 LAME STATUS ALERTS

Along with billions of other people, gay hearts are posting their status on Facebook and Twitter. They are also weeping at the stupid and quite ridiculous status alerts of their friends. While gay hearts think status alerts are a great idea for codependent couples to keep track of their whereabouts and actions every five minutes, they are not so sure about the rest of the world, because weepy lame status reports are popping up by the second:

Mike *has officially passed out.*

Amber *says a clean house is the sign of a broken TV.*

Sam *is sweating like a cat in a Chinese restaurant.*

Jake *is about to release my first sex tape with my beer gut and pasty white ass. Enjoy!*

Roco *What color would a Smurf turn if you choked it?*

Katie *Does anyone know how late Target is open?*

Bored at work *Why do they call it taking a dump if you are actually leaving a dump?*

David *Spell yo banana boy backwards.*

Jenn *is doing absolutely nothing today and is completely exhausted from it.*

Andrew *Can blind people see their dreams?*

Luvver *feels like getting some work done so he is sitting down until it passes.*

Lindsay *TGIF time for beer!*

Booyah *Just farted in Slinky's cubicle. It was so bad she threw up. Fire in the hole!*

Maddie *had my nails done. I feel so sparkly like Edward.*

Jason *is recommended by 4 out of 5 girlfriends and board-certified.*

While gay hearts weep over lame status alerts such as these, they'd also like to point out that, more often than not, these nuggets of nonsensical monotonous absurdity can provide quite the LOL. And that's what dumb friends are for.

⟨122⟩ DESIGNER SIGNATURE OVERLOAD

Gay hearts weep with fashion revulsion when they see people sporting no fewer than four different kinds of designer signature prints crashing into each other like an alphabet Armageddon. Are these people blind? Do they not see how ridiculous they look? Gay hearts feel that anyone strutting down the street coated in a variety of clothing and accessories stamped with Coach Cs, Louis Vuitton LVs, Gucci Gs, Fendi Fs, Chanel Cs, and Burberry's plaid should immediately be covered with a giant black garbage bag and whisked away to a secret location where they will be stripped of their designer signature overload and shipped off to fashion boot camp. There they will be taught how to dress better and properly use designer signatures for accenting, not bathing in. It's really the only way to protect the public from these fashion eyesores and keep the weeping to a minimum.

123 THE UBIQUITOUS SCARF

Weeping gay hearts want to know what is up with the threadbare ubiquitous scarf becoming a year-round fashion accessory staple worn with everything from bathing suits and shorts to sport coats and jumpsuits and looking like the wearer just tore up some hideous fabric they found in the trash and draped it around their neck. Gay hearts would like to tell everyone PLEASE JUST STOP WEARING SCARVES IN THE MIDDLE OF SUMMER! You look ridiculous at the barbecue in flip-flops and shorts sporting a yellow plaid *Lawrence of Arabia* neck sash look waiting for your camel to show up. Bring your scarves out to wear when the weather turns chilly and your neck needs that warm cozy feeling—when they are supposed to be worn. And when it comes to those Palestinian-inspired scarves with checks and tassels, please keep this in mind: Hobo Chic is one of the worst fashion trends in recent memory, and you should not be attempting to bring it back. There's only one place the ubiquitous scarf should be headed: retirement.

124 BAD HYGIENE

Gay hearts pride themselves on looking and smelling fresher than the Orbit chewing gum girl, so whenever they encounter a person with bad hygiene, they weep while pinching their nose and trying not to vomit from the rotting cabbage smell. Gay hearts are also weeping over the concept of bad hygiene because it seems to be a stinky trend among younger straight males. *Twilight* heartthrob Robert Pattinson shouted out to the whole world in an interview on *Extra* he doesn't think he needs to wash his hair or clean his apartment. It's rumored he went six weeks without putting suds in his rat nest, saying "I don't really see the point in washing your hair." This kind of statement coming from a Hollywood actor makes gay hearts weep even more and wonder what is up with publicists?

But wait! It gets worse. Pig Pen Pattinson also said if you are staying the night at his pad, you'd better be prepared for a filthy apartment as well: "If you don't care if your hair's clean or not then why would you wash it? It's like I don't clean my apartment 'cause I don't care. I have my apartment for sleeping in and I have my hair for just, you know, hanging out on my head. I don't care if it's clean or not." And as can be expected, someone who doesn't wash their hair or clean their apartment, will more than likely smell like moldy corn chips. Several sources who worked with Pig Pen on *New Moon*, exposed the actor's lazy hygiene habits, saying, "He stinks. I mean, it's awful. He never showers, and it drives people on the set crazy." A second crew member added: "He completely reeks!" Weepy grossed out gay hearts are so relieved Pig Pen is not playing on their team after discovering this tragic, wrenching news. Because if he were, he'd be thrown back to the straights so fast, his body odor wouldn't have time to catch up. Of course he'd be doused in Febreze first, but the gay hearts would definitely toss him back.

(125) BEING POOR

A gay heart + being poor = lots and lots and lots of poor gay heart weeping. The poor gay heart does not do so well because many of their friends make decent livings. This and stubborn pride causes him to often fib about being poor.

TEN THINGS GAY HEARTS HATE ABOUT BEING POOR:

1. Not being able to afford Starbucks or drinks at other coffee houses. Weeping early-morning poor gay hearts need their caffeine fix but they will have to get it from less expensive places, like 7-Eleven or their old nasty coffeemaker, or, if they are really broke, drink it from the pot brewed at work.
2. Having to lie to their friends about not being able to go drinking at swanky hot spots. If a poor gay heart is out with friends and they are headed to a swanky hot spot, he suddenly has to feign food poisoning.
3. Not being able to shop at Target, Trader Joe's, or Whole Foods, and having to instead spend their little bit of cash at the 99 Cent Store, Big Lots, 7-Eleven, and a neighbor's garage sale.
4. Having to ask parents or relatives for money, which is followed by a forty-five-minute lecture that will undoubtedly leave poor gay hearts depressed and wanting to get shitfaced. Since they are poor they will have to do it with Popov vodka.
5. Not having enough cash for lunch and having to mooch off friends. The gay heart will tell the friend he left his wallet at home.
6. Having to cut and dye their own hair. If his poor gay hearts ruin their mops, they have no choice but to lie and tell all their friends the expensive salon down the street did it and they are never going back!
7. Not being able to afford exotic vacations like many of their friends. When asked where they are going a poor gay heart will usually use a relative in a city to make his vacation sound more glamorous: "I'm going to a fancy spa in Chicago! Can't wait!"

TEN THINGS GAY HEARTS
HATE ABOUT BEING POOR:

8. Always having to buy the cheap knock-off store brand because poor gay hearts can't afford the real brand.
9. Missing movies, concerts, and Broadway shows and then having to pretend that they actually went: "Madonna was amazing! I got sprayed with her sweat!"
10. Having to buy all their clothes at Walmart or resale shops. Like all discount store shopping, this is a challenge for gay hearts, but if they get lucky and they're complimented, they'll definitely say, "Oh, this old thing? I bought it at Sak's a few seasons ago."

No matter how poor a gay heart is, he will go to great lengths to look like money and never let *anyone* see him weep about it on the outside.

STUPID PEOPLE

As Forrest Gump says, "Stupid is as stupid does," and whenever gay hearts encounter stupid people they weep to keep
from slapping them. As much as they try to avoid stupid
people, getting caught in the clutches of some dumbass never
fails and gay hearts stumble across stupid people all over the
place. For example . . .

- at work, where they ask
  the same question over
  and over
- on the freeway, where
  they merge into the fast
  lane then slow down to
  10 miles an hour
- in the elevator, where
  they push the button of a
  floor already lit up
- at the mall, where they
  hold up the line at the
  coffee kiosk because
  they just don't under-
  stand the sizes on the
  menu board

The world is full of stupid people doing stupid things every
second of the day, whether they're fixing things with duct tape,
trying to steal a two-liter bottle of Coke by shoving it down
their pants, asking a salesperson if everything is on sale when
it's not, or running a country with half a brain. A gay heart will
be right behind these idiots, shaking her head and weeping for
them to start using their brains.

127 TOO MUCH ED HARDY

When Ed Hardy first came onto the fashion scene, gay hearts welcomed the funky-colored tattoo-influenced clothing line because the artwork was cool, artsy, and unique. The weeping began when reality star and daddy of eight Jon Gosselin was spotted wearing Ed Hardy everywhere all the time. Things went downhill from there. Mainstream bought into it at lightning speed and everyone from the Jersey Shore kids to Beverly Hills bitches to soccer moms were sporting Christian Audigier–designed Ed Hardy baseball caps, flip-flops, belts, tops, or whatever they could get their hands on.

But having just one piece of Ed Hardy, like tennis shoes or a T-shirt, was not enough for many Hardy fans. The fashion-tards had to go and overdose on Ed Hardy and start wearing it from head to toe! For a long time it was a normal occurrence to see a woman at the airport wearing an Ed Hardy tracksuit with an Ed Hardy baseball cap, Ed Hardy Chucks, and an Ed Hardy tote bag. Gay hearts wept in horror when this awful fashion overload trend hit the streets, and many of them began purging their Ed Hardy pieces as thrift store donations. The saturation of Ed Hardy has gone the way everything popular goes in today's world of consumption—an overload of unnecessary merchandise emblazoned with his name, from body lotion to drinking glasses to totally random shit like mini electric toy airplanes. Gay hearts say good riddance to Ed. Fashion-tard Jon Gosselin can have him. We've got Marc Jacobs and there's no weeping there.

(128) NOT BEING ABLE TO DANCE

Whenever a person says she can't dance, there will be a gay heart nearby weeping to the beat. He will immediately make it his life's mission to get the DJ to play any Madonna or Lady Gaga song so he can drag the dancing-handicapped nervous soul onto the dance floor and teach her how to boogie like a YouTube star. For gay hearts, not being able to dance is like not being able to walk. While there are those people who are self conscious about gettin' down on the dance floor, the other side of the weepy dance coin are the folks who think they can kill a move like Michael Jackson, but they're actually well on their way to killing people next to them with their flailing arms and legs, not unlike Elaine Benes from *Seinfeld*, whose bad dancing was comparable to a chicken dry-heaving.

If you find yourself at a club dancing, look out for these weepy dancers:

The No Rhythm Dancer: Someone who is having a blast and wanting to be the life of the party. Think they're a fantastic shaker (like Elaine), but the arms, legs, and ass are not exactly in sync with the beat. The No Rhythm Dancer is all over the dance floor and has such erratic moves, they tend to fall, trip, lose their shoes, and crash into other dancers. Entertaining to watch; dangerous to dance next to.

The Acting-Out Dancer: Gay hearts weep with laughter over this bad dancer. The Acting-Out Dancer does exactly that—acts out the words or copies moves from a famous dance video. These dancers are usually completely trashed, but they can be super entertaining to watch!

The Hump and Grinder: These are the dudes who think they've got their charisma as well as their moves down to go right into bumping and grinding with any girl. Problem is, they don't know what the hell they're doing and most of the time they end up getting smacked.

The Blast from the Past Type: Here we have retro dancers popping out with the Moonwalk, Running Man, and Cabbage Patch and trying to get everyone else into the Electric Slide. They probably used to be something hot on the dance floor, maybe a decade or two ago, but never bothered to upgrade their moves. While they're busting out these ancient dance moves, they'll take up the whole dance floor, so good luck if you felt like dancing too.

The Stripper Pole Type: This is the chick who thinks she can pull off sexy moves on the dance floor (with or without a pole) but in actuality she is a complete stripper fail. This bad dancer always wants to be the star, the center of attention, so she'll put on her best moves and try to work it. It's okay to laugh when she falls and busts her drunk ass.

(129) FANNY PACKS

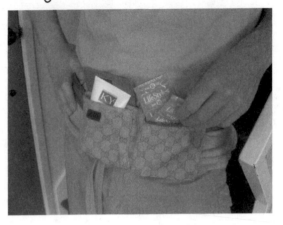

They can change the name and call them waist pouch, waist bag, pouch pockets, or mini carryall; they can be reproduced by famous designers like Fendi, Prada, Coach, and Louis Vuitton; they can be updated by well-known outdoor performance clothes manufacturers like North Face and Patagonia; and they can end up on must-have hot lists for the millionth time. But for gay hearts, when it comes to FANNY PACKS, a weepy ugly duckling is still a weepy ugly duckling even if it's made by Gucci and strapped on Sarah Jessica Parker in *Sex and the City*.

Fanny packs are one of the worst accessories ever invented in the history of fashion, and gay hearts weep synthetic tears whenever they see one of the little waist monsters that always make those who wear them look like they're packing a mountain climbing survival kit. They make gay hearts want to grab a pair of gardening shears and cut them off every person they see sporting one, whether it's a skinny model, one of their friends, or a chunky soccer mom—no one looks good in one! Since many of the culprits keeping fanny packs alive seem to be high-end fashion designers who every year or so reproduce them in new shapes and colors and re-market their heinous-ness as a seasonal must-have, gay hearts would like to introduce a campaign that will hopefully make these designers think twice about forcing recycled tired '80s fashion on the world. It's time everyone stood up and said NO to this fashion monstrosity once and for all with "No Fanny Pack Zone." Women do not need to have a utility belt around their waist drawing attention to their hips, and men do not need to look like geeky German tourists. C'mon Gucci, Prada, Fendi, and Louis V, what do you say? Start a waist-pouch revolution. Join the No Fanny Pack Zone. You'll be glad you did and so will the millions of fanny-pack wearing people who will suddenly realize the errors of their fashion disaster ways and never assault the public with their fanny packs again.

GAY BRIDEZILLAS

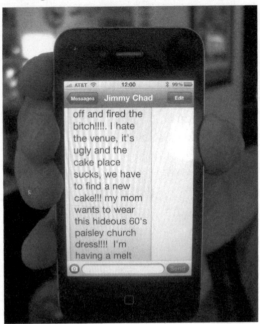

As more and more gay hearts head to the altar, the weeping over planning and executing of gay weddings will reach epic meltdown status—especially if two Bridezillas are marrying each other!

To keep from weeping, be aware of a gay heart on the road to Bridezilla . . .

TEN SIGNS A GAY HEART
HAS BECOME A BRIDEZILLA

1. They have fired and rehired the wedding planner no fewer than five times, changed the food menu three times, switched cake flavors four times, bitched out the venue manager twice, and slapped the videographer.
2. A professional writer is hired to write, edit, and coach the vows so they won't be screwed up during the ceremony. However, the Bridezilla has failed to mention to their partner that said writer is also a TV producer with the Logo channel and now the wedding is going to be a reality show.
3. They threaten to cancel the entire wedding if Marc Jacobs isn't somehow hunted down and forced to design the entire wedding party's clothes.
4. They make everyone re-enact the ceremony rehearsal more times than James Cameron.
5. They can't decide on what Fluffy and Apricot will wear to the wedding so they have ordered ten outfits from three different doggy boutiques.
6. At the gay bridal shower, they hand out sealed thank you notes and have guests address the envelopes to themselves. (Bridezilla claims it's saving time).
7. They demand pre-approval with options to veto what in-laws and their own parents are wearing to the wedding.
8. A CD of Melissa Etheridge singing "Come to My Window" is not enough; it has to BE Melissa Etheridge singing "Come to My Window."
9. By 12 P.M. the day of the wedding they have screamed and yelled at everyone within a few feet away. This would include Fluffy and Apricot. A massage, two martinis, and a Xanax are not helping.
10. They end up dancing to *Bad Romance* on the banquet table half naked while drinking champagne out of a dress shoe (or high heel) and enticing everyone to join them.

131 DRUNK TEXTING

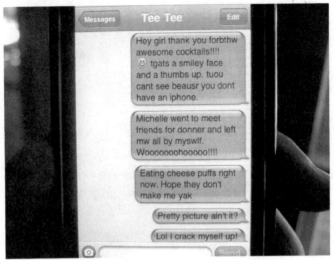

One day there will be legislation passed that prohibits people from texting and drinking at the same time. Until that day, drunk gay hearts will weep tears of regret with every character they type into their cell phone, because they know the next day they'll be slapping themselves for . . .

- Telling the boss to F off.
- Letting their best friend know they're angry over something that happened in high school—ten years ago.
- Breaking up with their boyfriend . . . twenty times in twenty minutes.
- Hitting the wrong keys and sending texts that look like this: *ltyl. ix0fucwq ←o...:(hat.*
- Coming clean about an embarrassing health issue and blasting the entire address book.
- Texting dirty words to mom and dad.
- Texting an ex from three years ago and telling them "I miss you and want you back."
- Texting the stalker they took a restraining order against and telling him "I miss you and want you back."
- Sending a booty call request to a roommate.
- Sending a booty call request to grandma.
- Accidentally blasting their entire address book about a hookup in the nightclub bathroom.
- Trying to read someone else's drunk text.

132 HAVING A BAD HAIR DAY

Nothing makes gay hearts weep more than when their hair just isn't doing what it's supposed to be doing. That's when coworkers or neighbors will say, "Dude, what's up with your hair? Did you do something different?" If not already aware of the hair scare, the gay heart will freak, pray to the gay hair gods it's not as horrendous as Phil Spector's electrical bouffant 'do, and find a mirror as fast as possible to see what kind of disaster is happening on top of his head. He will then attempt an emergency fix with their finger and spit (*only* if combs and products aren't available). Bad hair days happen to everyone, but gay hearts tend to be more emotional and weepy about how their hair looks at any given moment. If they've received a horrible haircut or color, social outings that can't be attended wearing a cap or stylish fedora are canceled and in some severe cases a gay heart has been known to even call in sick to work, refuse to leave the house, or cancel a hot booty call because of misbehaving hair. However, the good news for many gay hearts about bad hair days is that because of current hairstyle trends inspired by that just-awakened-and-rolled-out-of-bed look known to many as "bed head," almost anyone can go anywhere with bad hair and most people won't have a clue. They'll just think the tousled choppy mess was done on purpose at a high-end salon, and this makes a gay heart happy!

WEEPIEST HAIRSTYLES

- Man bangs
- Afro
- Bowl cuts
- The Mullet
- The modified Mullet
- Wisped fairy
- Peacock scene hair
- Buzzed cuts in patterns
  and mazes
- Big '80s hair
- Ratty hippie hair
- Dad cut (semi-bald with hair
  on the sides)
- Soccer Mom cut (short with
  long bangs parted to the side)

- Shoulder locks that look like Medusa snakes (from cheap chain haircuts)
- Feathered hair
- Hair bumps

133 SHIRT VIOLATIONS

As with pants and shoes, gay hearts weep over insidious shirts that should not be worn where people are milling about. Gay heart shirt violations will be issued for:

- Tube tops
- Redneck shirts with sleeves torn out
- Sequins and rhinestones on anything that's not evening wear
- T-shirts with wolves howling at the moon
- Flannel shirts
- Crop tops
- Super low V-necks
- Tanks tops that look like they were designed for an 8-year-old
- Denim shirts
- Popped collars on polo shirts
- Popped collars on men's clubbing shirts
- Shirts that make you look like you have full-sleeve arm tattoos
- Novelty sweater and sweat tops
- Shirts with giant flames
- Shirts with shoulder pads
- Ruffled poet shirts
- Billowy silk shirts
- Pajama shirts

134 ENERGY DRINK CRASHES

Many gay hearts go from their morning coffees right into their afternoon energy drinks, and they have no idea how the pioneer settlers survived without these pick-me-up enhancements. But sometime late in the afternoon, the wiry buzz that had been keeping them electrified and feeling like Spiderman starts to fade and burn out. Energy Drink Crash— EDC—sets in. And when that happens, gay hearts are too tired to even weep as they look for a place to rest their head, like a supply closet.

EDC affects millions of people every day; it usually starts at around 4 in the afternoon when most sufferers are at work. The first signs of EDC are thirst, dry mouth, weakness, and dizziness. A gay heart may think these symptoms are from the crush they have on a hot newbie coworker, so the symptoms can go unnoticed for a while as they nervously try to figure out if he's gay and single. Advanced symptoms include: increased heart rate and body temperature, decreased sweating and urination, muscle cramps, nausea, and tingling in hands and feet. Again, a gay heart may attribute these feelings to what's going on at work, especially if drama is involved and they got into it with the bitch from HR about the time off they need for Gay Days at Disneyland.

What may follow next are the more severe EDC symptoms of muscle spasm, vomiting, confusion, seizures, dim vision, racing pulse, and in some extreme conditions unconsciousness. At this point if the gay heart doesn't completely pass out, they realize all of these sensations must be EDC. At which point they must make a decision: Do they stay and keep flirting with hot newbie, go home sick, or pop open a Red Bull and keep going. Most opt for the Red Bull because it will give them that chatty high which they'll need to find out more about hot newbie.

135 ENTITLED DUMBASSES

It's not enough the world is filled with stupid people, but there now exists an entire group of morons who are not only dumbasses, but overcome with the self-centered condition known as entitlement complex. This ignorant "me" mentality has spread across America like a virus and gay hearts weep for those people who think they are entitled to getting their way above everyone else.

Entitled Dumbasses are especially dangerous because while they are expecting the world to revolve around them, they have their ends up their asses, and they are not paying attention to anything that does not interest them. Take for instance the rich lady dripping in designer clothes who walks into a boutique store and decides to hang her umbrella on a fire alarm switch because she did not want to set it on the ground while she took off her coat. The alarm went off and she ignored it, oblivious. Three fire trucks showed up and the store was fined $500. The lady continued shopping without a care in the world. Gay hearts would like to tell entitled dumbasses like that to wake the hell up! Smell the coffee beans and take a look around. Open your self-centered eyes! You are not the only person on this planet and you need to start using the brain cells God gave you. C'mon now. Really? Get with the program. The red zone is not your private parking spot.

136 NOT GETTING PICKED FOR RUPAUL'S DRAG RACE

DRAG RACE AUDITIONS

Many gay heart drag queen wannabes weep because they will never get to be on RuPaul's fabulous *Drag Race* TV show on Logo. This would be because they have no drag skills whatsoever. They are lousy lip-synchers, can't put together costumes, can't do makeup or fit into women's clothes, wear high heels, walk a catwalk in heels and they definitely can't dance! The life of drag is only possible for a select few with the queen's gift. Even though queenless gay hearts dream of doing drag, they would probably not even get chosen for an initial audition. The drag competition would eat them alive.

But who wouldn't want to be America's next drag superstar under the watchful, inspirational guidance of the ever-fabulous RuPaul? As the queens get to prove their worth after the challenges, she says, "The time has come for you to lip-synch for your life!" and then she follows up with that announcement by saying, "Good luck and don't fuck up!" Two remaining queens face off by dancing and lip-synching to the same song. RuPaul chooses the better performance, telling the winner to "shante," while the loser gets to "sashay away." While a gay heart would weep at hearing the word "sashay," he'd still be happy that he got that far. Secretly, everyone wants to be a drag queen.

137 WHITE TRASH FOOD

Most white trash food makes gay hearts weep for several reasons. If it doesn't remind them of a Wonder Bread childhood they're trying to forget, they are completely repulsed by the unhealthy and processed ingredients most of it has. On the trashy flip side, however, if a gay heart is at a White Trash Trailer Park theme party dressed in cowboy boots, an XXS wife beater, and Daisy-Duke cutoffs, and she's downed four Jell-O shots, drunk five Bud Lights, and smoked a doobie, the White Trash Food table will start to look like the deli section at Whole Foods. Not weeping at all, a gay heart White Trash Party goer will let her guard down and give in to trashed taste buds, even if she ends up paying for it the next morning.

Here's a list of Weepy White Trash Foods. Which one is your favorite?

- Finger sandwiches made with Wonder Bread, American cheese, and bologna, or peanut butter and banana
- Mac and cheese with chopped hot dogs on top
- Frito chili pie
- Chicken and dumplings
- Pork and beans with mini dogs
- Ritz crackers and Cheez Whiz
- Fried hot dogs, Spam, and Vienna sausages
- Fish sticks
- Bowls of pork rinds, Cheetos, Funyuns, and Granny Goose Potato Chips
- Twinkies, Ding Dongs, and Ho Ho's (contrary to what you might think, these are snack cakes, not a new Broadway show about Rentboys)
- Little Debbie cookies, cakes, and cupcakes
- Oreo cookie anything
- Ambrosia in a variety of gay rainbow colors
- Drinks: Bud, wine coolers, Hawaiian Punch, and Franzia in the box

As Paula Deen might say, "Come and get it, y'all!"

138 GETTING BUSTED FOR NOT GOING GREEN

The planet and its environment are important to all gay hearts and they do their best to keep up with conservation, recycling, and awareness, but they are only gay heart human and sometimes they slip. Maybe they waste a bit of electricity. Or they don't have a compost pile in their backyard. Or they take hour-long showers twice a day. Whatever the "not going green" rule is they break, they almost always attempt to do it without anyone noticing. This would be because they don't want to hear their friends or family correct them for keeping their place too hot or too cold, or be told they aren't doing enough to save the planet. They get it; they want to be a part of the solution and not the problem.

So they try their hardest. Until they get busted by a neighbor who spots them throwing their water bottle in the regular garbage can instead of the blue recycle one. As the neighbor confronts them, they'll try to backpedal and say, "Oh, geez, silly me! I tossed it in the wrong container!" But the neighbor, who is a staunch environmentalist type (she has a compost pile and everything), is too smart for the green-washing gay heart and she opens the garbage can to retrieve the bottle and spots a whole slew of recycling crimes: water bottles, beer bottles, plastic containers, on and on. The gay heart attempts to backpedal and make up some bullshit about misplacing them, but this doesn't fly with Compost Connie, who proceeds to stand in the street and give a detailed thirty-minute lecture on why it's important to recycle. Let the green tears flow.

139 STAYCATIONS

Gay hearts love to travel! They don't care where they go—an exotic island in the Bahamas, a weekend trip to NYC, or Florida to play with Goofy at Disney's Resort. It doesn't matter where they travel as long as they get to see some exciting new scenery, meet hot people, have a fun-filled adventure, and maybe end up guzzling colorful drinks with umbrellas on a private island somewhere. Yes, gay hearts will go just about anywhere, even to visit the parents or in-laws in neighboring cities and states. The one place they're not fond of going is HOME.

Gay hearts weep like a whiny baby bitch if they are suddenly faced with having to spend their time off work as a staycation—staying home for a vacation. Since most gay hearts are not fond of staycations (because they already spend so many weekends at home working on the house or yard), they will try to make the most of it by planning fun events like bowling, going to the movies, sleeping, barbecues, bar-hopping, shopping, and having lots of sex. But the problem with most staycations revolves around being vulnerable to friends, family, and work. Family members could show up at the door with suitcases ready for *their* vacation! Or friends find out you are off and schedule so many things to do that you are exhausted by the time your staycation ends. And then there's the biggest staycation nightmare of all: Work knows you're home and calls you in to help. Poof. No more vacation. Only weeping, weeping, weeping! Because of these disadvantages, most gay hearts will only be able to handle one staycation a decade. As soon as the monotony of it ends, they vow to never be in that weepy vacation position again and immediately start saving for their dream trip to Australia.

VACATION DESTINATIONS THAT MAKE EVERY GAY HEART WEEP

The Bible Belt

Uganda

Cheap cruises

Iran

Alaska

Cross-country drives

Visits to homophobic in-laws

Wilderness camping

Going anywhere in a motor home

LOSING DESIGNER SUNGLASSES

Gay hearts have always had a love affair with designers. They love style and quality, so for them forking out $300 for a pair of amazing Gucci sunglasses is a normal everyday must-have purchase. But when those little Gucci gems go missing, the gay heart goes into a weeping tantrum that would rival anything Elton John threw if any of his glasses went missing. (Although, on second thought, he's a super-rich gay and can buy loads of $300 Gucci sunglasses so they'd get replaced instantly without so much as an afterthought . . . unlike the average gay heart who maxed out his credit card to purchase the glasses in the first place.) After calming down over the loss of Gucci fabulousness, the gay heart then makes a reluctant decision. It's a decision they have no control over and one that they've had to do many times before. With a shudder and a twitch they begrudgingly head to the mall, where they find a little sunglasses kiosk with a sign that says *Everything $10*. Feeling sad and very weepy, the gay heart will buy five pairs while saying, "It's okay, this is only temporary. One day Gucci will find my face again."

141 KNOCK-OFF DESIGNER WEAR

Since gay hearts are nearly one with the fashion industry, it should come as no surprise they weep at the sight of knock-off designer clothes. Gay hearts believe if you want to wear the likes of Louis Vuitton, Chanel, or Gucci it should be the real thing, not some poorly constructed copy.

While not everyone can afford to dress like they just stepped off the runway, gay hearts can understand why some would want to buy fake designer handbags off a bedsheet on a sidewalk in the middle of Times Square, or head to Chinatown's Canal Street and discover a shop's secret room through a trap door loaded with more knock-off fashion bounty than *Vogue* magazine's closet. And even though gay hearts feel it's weepy to buy "fake" anything, often they will get caught up in the excitement of knock-off shopping themselves.

While most can afford a piece or two of fabulous designer wear (bought on sale), many gay hearts succumb to the thrill of buying fake stuff because of bartering. There's nothing like haggling over a fake $50 Louis Vuitton and trying to get it down to the $30 in cash they're waving around like hundred-dollar bills. Knock-off sellers are hungry for a buck and they'll end up taking the $30 and attempt to sell the matching wallet for $25. A gay heart shopping on Canal Street can easily resemble a gay heart shopping at a Barney's sale. But what makes a gay heart really weep, and even pisses her off a little bit, is when someone wearing a bunch of knock-off duds runs around bragging to everyone that it's real. This is so wrong to weeping gay hearts, and they want to say to these fashion fibbers "Be proud of your $25 fake Coach bag and tell the truth! Many will be in awe over the great price you paid!" (As long as it's not a cop questioning you coming out of the back room of a shop in Chinatown.)

(142) PIGGY PEOPLE

You will never see gay hearts littering, making a mess at a restaurant, decimating a bathroom, or ruining merchandise in a store, but when they witness piggy people doing these things, pillaging the neighborhood like out-of-control barbarians, they weep with disgust (while helping to clean up because they can't believe people behave this way). Because so many gay hearts work in the service industry as, among other things, waiters, cashiers, or salespeople, they have had to deal firsthand with piggy people and their children inconsiderately making merchandise messes across stores and fitting rooms, opening food packages in grocery stores (then eating from them and putting them back on the shelf), spilling drinks and food everywhere, throwing containers of half-eaten fast food out their car windows, and basically just committing one filthy piggish act after another. Gay hearts have had it with these piggy bitches and are mobilizing to create a group called "Piggy People Prevention!" that will fight for tougher laws against the pigs roaming the cities and towns of America. Piggy people caught breaking "pig laws" will be forced to clean up their mess immediately and sentenced to a year of cleaning up the messes other piggies have made. Then they will all be sent to Pig Island where they can thrive and roll around in the filthiness they love to create, safely away from their neater gay heart counterparts.

(143) HUGH JACKMAN IS NOT GAY

Photo by Grant Brummett

And boy gay hearts weep, because besides being an incredibly smoking-hot man, Hugh Jackman is an actor, singer, performer, gay rights supporter, dad, husband, and all-around amazing person. What gay heart would not want him to be gay? Hugh has been assailed with the "Are you gay" question for years, most notably because he starred on Broadway playing a gay man (Peter Allen in *The Boy from Oz*), and many people felt he must be gay if he can sing, dance, act, kick to high heaven, and then turn around and do a butch action role like Wolverine all while looking hot as hell. But many gay hearts who believe he is straight cheer him for staying true to himself (as long as he really *is* straight). Hugh has been a strong supporter of gay rights and said in interviews that if he were gay, he would come out because denying it implies shame. Everything he's done on film or stage has left many gay heart boys melting with admiration. So gay heart boys weep for Hugh Jackman because he does not play on their team. But they want him to know if he ever changes his mind, he is more than welcome to join the gay hearts any time! For now they'll settle for those steamy TMZ photos of him coming out of the ocean looking like Adonis.

(144) ANGELINA JOLIE IS NOT GAY

Photo by Gage Skidmore

And girl gay hearts weep, because besides being an incredibly smoking-hot woman, Angelina Jolie is an actress, humanitarian, gay rights supporter, mother, wife, and an all-around amazing person. What gay heart would not want her to be gay? Having a gay brother and also having been known for dabbling in bisexuality, Angelina Jolie has been an icon to the gay community for decades.

She has been a staunch supporter of gay rights and marriage, and her man Brad even said in an interview that they would not get married until it was legal for *everyone* to get married. Whether or not they can hold out that long will remain to be seen, but the sentiment warmed many a gay heart. Since they can't have her as a lesbian, gay heart girls are thrilled to at least have Angelina as a supporter. But they want her to know that if she ever changes her mind, she is more than welcome to join the gay hearts any time! For now they'll settle for watching this honorary gay heart kick-ass and look gorgeous on the silver screen while doing it.

CELEBS THAT GAY HEARTS WISH WOULD SWITCH TEAMS

Pamela Anderson

Alec Baldwin

Cate Blanchett

Bono

Gerard Butler

Steve Carell

Bradley Cooper

Daniel Craig

Zooey Deschanel

Tina Fey

Kathy Griffin

Jake Gyllenhaal

Demi Moore

Cyndi Lauper

Justin Long

MORE CELEBS THAT GAY HEARTS WISH WOULD SWITCH TEAMS

Joel McHale

Ellen Page

Brad Pitt

Natalie Portman

Ryan Reynolds

Ryan Seacrest

Meryl Streep

Barbra Streisand

Charlize Theron

Wendy Williams

Catherine Zeta-Jones

145 FIXING THINGS WITH DUCT TAPE

Gay hearts shake their heads and weep when they see cars, chairs, golf clubs, eyeglasses, and other broken items fixed with silver duct tape. Duct tape has become so popular for quick fixes it's now made in a variety of colors and prints, including hot pink, leopard, and camouflage. Fashion colors aside, gay hearts will toss out their broken floor lamp before they cover it with ugly silver tape. The only time a gay heart will ever use duct (with the exception of construction) is for his redneck Halloween costume.

146 CHEAP CRUISES

Gay hearts and cruises go together like sun and surf! They love all kinds of cruises—cruises to the Caribbean, cruises for all men, cruises for all women, cruises for gay couples, cruises through Alaska, cruises to the Bahamas, cruises on the fancy Queen Mary 2, and even family cruises put on by Disney (they cope with the kids or bring their own). Yes, nothing makes gay hearts happier than being out on the open seas while poolside with a Cosmo in their hand as they dream of all the amazing food they will gorge themselves with at dinner. So it's no surprise when a friend calls up and says, "Hey, there's a total bargain on this cruise to Mexico, we should go!" Hearing only the words "cruise to Mexico" and not really considering what the word "bargain" means in the cruise world, eager gay hearts will immediately reply with a "Hell, yeah! I'm on the way to look for a new swim suit!"

The weeping won't start until they board the bargain cruise and discover small, stinky, confined quarters, tacky hotel décor, limited cheap booze served in plastic cups, no shows to watch, horrible diarrhea-inducing buffet food, strange creepy redneck people, packs of unruly children screaming and yelling, no day spa or movie theater, bad plumbing and water pressure, creaking noises like the ship is falling apart, and a stomach flu virus that will force them to sleep by the small cramped toilet. A cheap cruise for gay hearts is a lesson learned about how there are some things in life you just shouldn't try to save money on. And cruises are one of them! If a gay heart feels a hankering to be on a deck looking out over water while saving money, it will be done on the Mark Twain riverboat at Disneyland, not on a dirty clown boat headed to Mexico.

147 BAD WEAVES

As mentioned earlier, gay hearts are quite sensitive to bad hair and when they see a bad weave job that looks like the chick was an extra in the movie *The Birds* and got really roughed up by a flock of seagulls, they weep for the ratty hair nest that remains on the top of her head. Bad weaves are everywhere—at the airport, the mall, the gym, walking down the street—and the more bad weaves a gay heart sees, the more scared they are. They want to know if there's some sort of bad weave pandemic going on. How could so many women NOT KNOW they have bad weaves? Aren't they looking in the mirror? Has no one told them their weaves are unraveling before everyone's eyes? Gay hearts weep for these women and want to help them, so they've set up an emergency toll-free number: 1-888-REPAIR MY WEAVE. Anyone who spots a weave that looks like it's going to attack a small child, please report it immediately!

148 THE DEATH OF MYSPACE

Dear MySpace:

Gay hearts everywhere would like to thank you. You were the first social network of your kind and we loved being a part of Internet history with you. Even though you are owned by Rupert Murdoch (see Fox News entry), gay hearts thank you for everything you did to get social-izing going online. They will never forget all you brought into their lives—the friends, lovers, and hookups; the slow-loading pages full of glitter graphics; the stupid bulletins clogging up inboxes; the bazillion ads; spyware and spam everywhere; the annoying music players; the constant barrage of musical acts want-ing to befriend you . . . and let's not forget the gaggle of nasty viruses that would pop up more often than not. It sure was fun, MySpace, wasn't it? Pioneering through the wilds of social networking together. Thankfully, gay hearts no longer have to go onto your site and weep about all those things that were once part of their daily lives. They have found a new friend to socialize with, a friend that's more user friendly! His name is Facebook, and he's not perfect by a long shot, but way, way ahead of you. There's also this girl Twitter who is lots of fun to be around. She's pretty easy also. It seems the end may be near for you, MySpace. There's no way of telling, really, but gay hearts everywhere wanted to tell you it's been fun and it's been real, but they're glad they don't have to weep over you anymore.

CHER'S LAST SHOW

One thing all gay hearts agree on is they LOVE Cher! Besides looking stunningly beautiful and making music that has gay hearts singing and dancing, Cher has been iconic to gays forever. She has been imitated by drag queens, performed in front of millions of gay hearts across the world, and had her birthday celebrated like a national holiday at gay bars playing her music.

Cher also lovingly supported her daughter who had surgery to become a man. During her son Chaz's sex change, Cher said, "The one thing that will never change is my abiding love for my child." Gay impressionist Jimmy James has this quote about Cher's longevity and inspiration: "After a nuclear holocaust all that will be left are cockroaches and Cher!"

Goddess to gay hearts, Cher transitioned from dance music to social activism in the last decade and has become one of the gay community's most vocal advocates. She was honored with a GLAAD Media Award (Gay and Lesbian Alliance Against Defamation), the *Advocate* named her one of the "25 Coolest Women," and the Bravo program *Great Things About Being . . .* declared Cher the number one greatest thing about being gay.

In April 2005, 18,000 fans packed the Hollywood Bowl for what was being called Cher's last concert. Many were sad and there was lots of weeping, but here we are years later and Cher is still performing in amazing places like Las Vegas. This makes gay hearts everywhere very happy. But make no mistake about it—when Cher does have her *real* last show, gay hearts will weep for all eternity. They will miss their gaylicious diva, but keep her in their gay hearts forever.

150 GAY PRIDE LETDOWN

Gay pride is one event that brings gay-heart boys and gay-heart girls and all their friends and family together in gay solidarity. It's a day many gay hearts look forward to all year, and as the parade roars down the street under the summer sun with colors of the rainbow and emotional cheers for floats, organizations, community leaders, and parents of gays, the gay hearts are filled with love, acceptance, and camaraderie. They gather by the thousands to bond together, witness the advances in their community, and celebrate the life of a gay heart. After the parade, many flock to a festival where everyone eats, drinks, dances, and frolics under the sun. As with any awesome day, it must come to a close and gay hearts must take their drunken, tired, sunburned, hoarse bodies home. Filled with images and voices of the day, they weep rainbow colors for gay pride letdown. It's not a sad weep, but a proud, hopeful, loving weep. And with warm gay heart smiles, they look forward to next year.

QUIZ: HOW WEEPY IS YOUR GAY HEART?

Check the box if the item makes your gay heart weep—even a little bit! Then count how many things make you weepy.

☐ Bad Drag
☐ Facebook Gifts
☐ Cheap Booze
☐ A Town Without Target, Trader Joe's, or Whole Foods
☐ Sarah Palin
☐ Manboobs
☐ Anything Having to Do with *Twilight*
☐ Crocs
☐ No Valet Service
☐ Scary Sex Toys
☐ People Who Don't Like to Be Called Hon, Sweetie, or Girl
☐ Overpriced Cupcakes
☐ Scary Packages
☐ Tap Water
☐ Nouvelle Cuisine
☐ Improper Usage of Uggs
☐ Couples Who Dress Alike
☐ *Jesus Camp* (the movie)
☐ Broken Gaydar
☐ Ass Cracks
☐ Richard Simmons
☐ Missing the Oscars
☐ Crocheted Accessories
☐ Bad Kissers
☐ Expensive Drinks
☐ The Snuggie Blanket
☐ Nicholas Sparks Books and Movies
☐ Having to Take a Bus Anywhere
☐ Bad Wine
☐ A Wii Fit Collecting Dust
☐ No Internet Access

- ☐ Sideways Trucker Hats
- ☐ Manorexia
- ☐ Instant Coffee
- ☐ Knock-off Porn
- ☐ People Who Can't Park
- ☐ Overusing "OMG"
- ☐ Twitter Diarrhea
- ☐ M. Night Shyamalan Movies
- ☐ Slow Porn Downloads
- ☐ Stupid Gay T-shirts
- ☐ Chubby People in Tight Clothes
- ☐ Fugly Designer Clothes
- ☐ Justin Bieber
- ☐ Hat Violations
- ☐ Old Bars That Smell Like Piss
- ☐ Baggy Fleece Sweatsuits
- ☐ As Seen on TV Products
- ☐ People Who Want to Pop Other People's Zits
- ☐ Craigslist Liars
- ☐ Not Owning an iPhone
- ☐ Hipsters
- ☐ Capri Pants
- ☐ Dogs Costumes
- ☐ Having to Trap or Kill a Roach or Mouse
- ☐ Bad Tippers
- ☐ Ridiculous Fetishes
- ☐ Having to Get Up Before 9 in the Morning
- ☐ Taking a Bad Picture
- ☐ Bread Makes You Fat
- ☐ Fist-Bumping
- ☐ Venetian Blind Sunglasses
- ☐ Signing Up for a Gym and Never Using It
- ☐ Tacky Car Accessories
- ☐ Fashion Failures
- ☐ No Starbucks Within Walking Distance
- ☐ Junk Rooms

- ☐ Metrosexuals
- ☐ Trainwreck Britney
- ☐ Diets That Don't Work
- ☐ Wearing Flip-Flops with Socks
- ☐ Not Wearing a Halloween Costume
- ☐ Standing in Line
- ☐ Creepy Motels
- ☐ *True Blood* and *Dexter* Spoilers
- ☐ The Chicken Dance
- ☐ Shoe Violations
- ☐ Food Network Addiction
- ☐ The Texting-Challenged
- ☐ Not Owning a TV
- ☐ Taxidermy
- ☐ Living in a Bad Part of Town
- ☐ Muffin Tops
- ☐ Overpriced Coffee Drinks
- ☐ Too Much Auto-Tune
- ☐ The Kardashians
- ☐ People Who Don't Hug
- ☐ Getting Caught Wearing the Same Clothes Two Days in a Row
- ☐ Blackout Drinking
- ☐ Watching Madonna from the Nosebleed Section
- ☐ Ugly Tramp Stamps
- ☐ Hoarders
- ☐ Rainbow-Colored Food
- ☐ Cuddle Parties
- ☐ Kissy-Face Photos
- ☐ Credit Card Denied
- ☐ Not Being Able to Fit in Your Favorite Designer Jeans
- ☐ Celebrity Perfumes
- ☐ Getting to a Sale Too Late
- ☐ Bikram Yoga
- ☐ Fox News
- ☐ Pant Violations

- ☐ Real Housewives Withdrawal
- ☐ Too Much Plastic and Botox
- ☐ Tacky Home Décor
- ☐ Ugly Trophy Jackets
- ☐ Shopping from TV
- ☐ Closeted Cartoon Characters
- ☐ Bratty Unattended Kids
- ☐ Bad Karaoke
- ☐ Potlucks
- ☐ Visible Thongs
- ☐ Discount Store Shopping
- ☐ Moochers
- ☐ Emo Hair
- ☐ Creepy Old Men
- ☐ Disney Line-Cutters
- ☐ Virtual Pets
- ☐ Ugly Christmas Sweater Parties
- ☐ Guidos and Guidettes
- ☐ Lame Status Alerts
- ☐ Designer Signature Overload
- ☐ The Ubiquitous Scarf
- ☐ Bad Hygiene
- ☐ Being Poor
- ☐ Stupid People
- ☐ Too Much Ed Hardy
- ☐ Not Being Able to Dance
- ☐ Fanny Packs
- ☐ Gay Bridezillas
- ☐ Drunk Texting
- ☐ Having a Bad Hair Day
- ☐ Shirt Violations
- ☐ Energy Drink Crashes
- ☐ Entitled Dumbasses
- ☐ Not Getting Picked for *RuPaul's Drag Race*
- ☐ White Trash Food
- ☐ Getting Busted for Not Going Green

- [ ] Staycations
- [ ] Losing Designer Sunglasses
- [ ] Knock-off Designer Wear
- [ ] Piggy People
- [ ] Hugh Jackman Is Not Gay
- [ ] Angelina Jolie Is Not Gay
- [ ] Fixing Things with Duct Tape
- [ ] Cheap Cruises
- [ ] Bad Weaves
- [ ] The Death of MySpace
- [ ] Cher's Last Show
- [ ] Gay Pride Letdown

_____ divided by 50 _____ x 100 =

_____ % Your Heart Is Weeping

ABOUT THE AUTHOR

Freeman Hall has a huge gay heart and has waited his whole life to sound off on the stuff that makes it weep. Author of an acclaimed memoir of his experiences toiling in *Retail Hell*, he now spends his days running four popular blogs and dog-walking his neighbor's adorable canines. His weeping gay heart should in no way be confused with a lyric in a country ditty (though many of them do make it weep). He lives in Los Angeles, CA.

For more to cry about, check out *www.gayheartsweep.com*.